POETRY

POETRY

UEA MA
Creative Writing Anthologies
2021

CONTENTS

TIFFANY ATKINSON	Preface	VII
BHANU KAPIL	Foreword	IX
AMNA ALAMIR		2
CHLOE BETTLES		12
ELEANOR BURLEIGH		20
HETTY CLISS		26
ABIGAIL CRAIG		32
SAM DAVIDSON		36
ROSE FRANCKLIN		44
GABRIELLE GRIOT		50
ALEX HILLMAN		58
MAYA HOUGH		64
P B HUGHES		72
ELKE HUISMANS		82
ALEX INNOCENT		88
LAUREN KANIA		96
VIV KEMP		102
PRERANA KUMAR		112
SAM NEWCOMBE		118
MARIANA PEÑA FEENEY		126
CHRISTOPHER PERRY		134
MAX PURKISS		144
GEORGE RICHARDS		154
JESSE SMITH		162
TIM SNELL		170
KIERA SUMMER		176
TRISTAN·E		186
ALEX WOOD		196
Acknowledgements		203

TIFFANY ATKINSON
Preface

Prefaces are written with one eye to posterity, and anthologies (it occurs to me as I flick through the wonderfully various textures and structures of these poems) are a kind of geological core sample. This layered volume has been laid down by effort, imagination and resilience over a – let's not say *unprecedented* – *but* a very challenging year. It represents the slow crystallising of individual voices through and against the pressure and frictions of group work and collaboration. This is how enduring things get made. I am proud to see it, and I hope that the contributors are too.

While Bhanu Kapil, our UNESCO Poetry Fellow this year, has been asking the poets, *what do you burn to say?* I have kept returning to the question, *what else do you know?* This may be because we haven't enjoyed the casual proximity through which our idiosyncrasies and enthusiasms usually slip and collide; by which, in a phrase that now sounds almost archaic, we get to know each other. Perhaps physical isolation has just made my nosiness more overt. But also, poetry is all *about* what else we know, about what and how else we know things, and can put them. It speaks obliquely, not just in the rhetorical sense of Emily Dickinson's 'tell it slant', but at an odd angle to everyday events and understanding, refracted through the particular expertise, experience, passions, sightlines of the poet. The act of writing itself may also be precisely the space where we *find out* what we burn to say, what else we know. The poem is a small environment, an ecology, a way of thinking things through on fresh terms. When did we ever need fewer of those?

In a year where most of us have been regularly confined to rooms, it is worth recalling that the word *stanza* means just that: a room. More specifically, it means a standing-place, so probably a small room, a room-in-waiting, a waiting-room. We might say that we have spent a whole year living in stanzas. We might venture too that in our stanzas we have relied very much on the communicative and connective potential of lines. The stanza and the line both house and reach out; the poem is already a model of the tensions of containment and release, structure and expression. It is as structurally, emotionally, imaginatively resourceful as we have discovered ourselves to be. Take that, posterity. Take this.

Tiffany Atkinson
UEA, June 2021

BHANU KAPIL
Foreword

The Future of Poetry

In the mid to late spring of 2021, I had the pleasure of Zooming with many poets at the University of East Anglia.

We spoke about the body, which is to say, the relationship between the life you're actually living and what's on the page.

We spoke about the edge of the page in the way that other communities speak about terrain.

What moves or slips beneath the page, for example, in the moments that we stop writing, if only to lift our pen or our fingertip from the paper, or the outer material of our device?

Some ideas: water, mineral seams, a memory that isn't absorbed by anything and thus keeps falling, producing traces or stains.

In this thinking near writing, or with it, we found analogues to trauma and embodiment: gestures and encounters of many kinds. To generalise, this is what we spoke about when we spoke about poetry, and it's from the shape of this conversation that I could extend some thoughts, as I've been invited to do, on the future of poetry.

No, that's not possible.

It's the question I forgot to ask you when we met.

Where are you going? How will you/did you: arrive?

These questions fall differently in an era or historical present in which the open possibility of arrival is no longer available as a metaphor for what a book could be.

Perhaps the question I could ask or pose in this foreword, as a conduit to the future book, is the one I did manage to ask, in the first minutes of a masterclass I taught this spring. In fact, it's not my own question, but rather, a question asked by the sculptor-ceramicist (artist) Gina Adams, when she visited a poetry workshop I was teaching, about two years ago.

'What do you burn to say?'*

Pay attention to what you felt or knew when you heard this question for the first time.

Find a way to stay in contact with that glimpse, then move it through the materials of your work.

How?

The answer to this question is the only adequate response to the title of this foreword.

The future of poetry is gestural, circadian, blobby and real.

*[Please substitute, for the last line of this foreword, whatever it is you know, having answered these questions, or asked them, in your notebook, your heart, or at 7.45 pm on a Thursday evening in East Anglia in June, when it's raining. No, the sky is still a milky blue.]

Bhanu Kapil

This diverse anthology comprises the latest work from the 2021 cohort of poets studying UEA's renowned Creative Writing MA.

AMNA ALAMIR

Amna Alamir is a Kuwaiti writer who grew up in England and the Middle East. She writes about her experiences dealing with issues such as race, identity, and the female voice. Her poetic inspirations are E E Cummings, Charles Bukowski, and Pablo Neruda.

Amnaalamir92@gmail.com

Poems
Gunslinger
This is what remains
Salt and Vinegar
If You Should Stumble Across Me In The Barren Woods
It must be true

Gunslinger

I saw
an 'i'
execute a 'u'
and gangs of letters
came out gunslinging
a comma grew wings
grew feathers
grew tentacles
and instead of flying
pecked the shit out of my brain

punctuation is just rude

I don't know about you
but that's enough to make me
want to stop
shot
drop down my pen

I can't trust
my syntax
it menstruates—
what's that saying
saying
don't trust anything that bleeds
I bleed all the time
I bleed from my bones
and it's hard enough
being a woman
without leaving a trail
everywhere you go
that's why I stay home—

trace the vowels
leaking from my brainstem
lend me yours

and a towel
it's cold out here
in this songless town
where tongues are hung up
and melodies drown

I couldn't rhyme
if I wanted to
wrestle or
wrangle a bear
I can never decide
what to wear
my pride and
ass always look
fat
in everything—
you wear your rejection
in the knots of your ties
try changing a one-legged tyre
it makes me tired
listing things
I can't do now

I have lost
the love I had for you
left it
by a bus stop
behind a stack of old things
in an old box
in Mexico
I gave up
the gunslingers followed me
and I never paid your ransom

you are like those extra buttons
they hide
in cotton hearts
that nobody ever uses
but it's nice to know when you're there

This is what remains

The last text I ever sent you
is strung upon a tree branch
don't ask me how
I never put it there

my voice
cold frightened quivering
took shade behind a cardinal
its small flaming feathers
growing around me
with fleeting love
and anger.
A fledgling
forced to age
like my resentment.

The last words
I ever said to you
carried on its spine
c-shaped, puckering
like an open mouth
unsure of what to say.

Sea-shaped
I dug up your sorrys
I dragged them
to the bottom of the water
where they belong
wet and struggling

I buried my heart
where you can't find it.
Beneath the rocks and broken shells
debris
the remaining feathers
that cling to me.

There are times I wake up
at night
hear the fluttering of wings
so close so far
and wonder if anyone
will ever love me again
and my heart aches.

Salt and Vinegar

They warned me
of men wearing coats
in shadows
wearing shadows
in coats
behind bushes
and parked cars
far from trembling eyes
and closed hearts
that flicker and shut
with every beat.

You wear
your breasts
strapped low
like armour
the thinness of my skin
is fragile/ floating/ nothingness

you did not listen
when I gulped
no.
I held a packet of
salt and vinegar crisps
against my chest
that was my only armour—

Your perfume
is the scent
of my childhood
it smells
of creeping tulips
wet sandcastles
I built
one summer in Thailand
an undressed smile

the dribbling dry
foam
off an ice cream cone
shadow puppets
that pretend to dance
innocently
when it rains   it rains   it rains.

If You Should Stumble Across Me In The Barren Woods

Hooded and lonesome
untie the shrouds and the clouds
that walk among you and I will
gently open inviting you in.

Reach out with tender curiosity
your fingertips, feign a lasso out
of heartstrings and I will share
the taste of the ocean
the many travels I have bottled up
and tossed at perturbed sailors.

Where they turned their backs on me:
this is night country
this *isn't right* country
in the blackness
I am suffocating
this isn't my country.

My body is changing
has taken on your culture
and become momentarily ill.
There are parts of me
I had to give up, I lost
gave to you in exchange
for your acceptance.

I covered myself in barberries, ginger root, cardamom.
I am a rare sighting, now
beyond the star-shaped stars
that float like lucid ribbons
when it is time to die
the earth shivers.

It must be true

I suck cock
hacked into the spine
of my door
wrote into existence
so it must be so

I suck cock
come from a foreign land
where women wear their
tongues in shackles
dance in desperation
transport their words
through veins
and pump them out (in
secret) one
by one
like crying babies
waiting to be born.

I suck cock
even as a child I
hid in the cracks of pavements
I counted backwards
to stay in the past
I threw rocks
and broke glasshouses
to make tragic music
because then, my heart was
breaking too
and the earth ripped open
sheltered me under the dirt
of its skin.

I suck cock
is all they wrote
all I am

in jagged lines
letters turning away from each
other
in humiliation
seething seeping
                I am angry
like the birds that fly
north during winter
because they feel like it
and don't give a fuck about your
      social conventions

I suck cock
good and long and hard
and what are you going to do about it
now.

CHLOE BETTLES

Chloe Bettles grew up in Leicester but tells everyone she's a Northerner. From a performance poetry background, she was the winner of the 2019 UniSlam competition and longlisted for the Outspoken award. Her writing tackles the topic of mental illness in a (hopefully) humorous way.

chloebettleswriting@gmail.com

Poems
Hold Music
Dirty Talk
Henhouse
What Wasps Do
Catch 22
Don't Adjust

Hold Music

After your lover excuses themselves to the bathroom, but just
before you can tell the bartender you've actually stopped drinking
for good, you receive a text from a wrong number that reads:
'Don't do it. Not tonight.'
and the possibility behind the blinking ellipses makes you think this is:

A hurried text between friends as a final effort to cancel the surprise
party that they'd been planning for months, because during the distraction
on the car ride over to her house, the birthday girl cuddled up
to the sender and told them their company was all she wished for anyway.

'Don't do it. Not tonight – because right now my heart is a fairground,
and if everyone leaves I'm basically guaranteed a free ride.' Or is it:

A judgemental text from a first wife to the fading grip on her husband,
who right now is in a stranger's bed instead of their son's flute recital,
even though he wanted to play the drums, even though *he* promised
he'd be here tonight because forever obviously isn't good enough.

'Don't do it. Not tonight – because I left the door unlocked for you
and the later it gets the less safe I feel in the bed you made.' Or is it:

A frantic text from the shaky hands of an estranged sister checking
every bridge until she runs out of power, and patience, and petrol,
so, she crawls into a telephone box next to a service station
on her knees, praying that God's wrong just this one fucking time.

'Don't do it. Not tonight – because the note on the dresser is still wet
and bad things always seem to happen to us both after dark.'

So, you order that drink. And another. And win the pub quiz all about
missed opportunities, vomiting over your lover's freshly washed
hands as they catch you, but let you fall. As you try to tell them
that you're actually sorry this time, all they can muster in reply is:

'Don't do it. Not tonight.'

Dirty Talk

For the last time, I don't have rats in my apartment
they were there when I moved in, if anything
the rats have me   – I mean you   – I mean *us*

I mean think of our mutual friend the philosopher
who told me over many drinks that if you caught
an infinite number of monkeys and tied them to
an infinite number of keyboards and rationed
them enough infinities, eventually one of those
monkeys could recreate the entire discography
of Britney Spears and set in motion an infinite
loop of becoming each other's muses, like me
with you, and like my poetry you hate so much,

and like that hard-hitting 2007 documentary
Ratatouille, about the mouse who learned
to cook food at that fancy restaurant
in France with the fantastic Yelp reviews
and maybe one day I could take you there,
if you'll let me, because I could love you in Paris
and I could love you on The Planet of The Apes

because I love you right here right now
as we wait patiently for *our* vermin
to serve us both breakfast in bed.
Until then, let us sleep in our oven mitts.
Let us evolve into somethingness.
Let us fester with it.

Henhouse

One day you accuse a fox of eating all your chickens
so that night he sneaks back and eats your baby.
And in the morning taunts: 'did no one ever teach you
that it's rude to bite the hand that feeds off you?
And we both know I'm no chicken to a dare.'

You repaint the henhouse the colour of aged bones,
craft a scarecrow that only makes the magpies cackle
as you plant a handful of baby teeth in the garden
in hopes of growing a tree made of porcelain.
But nothing happens. And as you blister under
the harvest moon that keeps you hungry you consider
inviting the fox back around for dinner.

You wonder if this is how the chicken must
have felt the first time it crossed the road.

Or the last time.

Or the time it decided to stay home,
cuddled under the covers to escape
the chill of the open waiting window.

What Wasps Do

There are only two things I know for certain:
I do not believe in us. You snore.
Staring at the water stains on the ceiling
feeling something a lot like loathing
when you tell me over scrambled eggs:
*'I swallowed a bumble bee at a picnic once,
and now the sound of it haunts my throat.'*

I exorcise my insomnia with whale song,
stuff your pillow full of lavender
hoping to tempt out something
like the truth. At sunrise I furiously
unmake our bed, un-twin all your socks,
try and hate you on purpose only
for you to smile all sunny side up.

A dead wasp floats atop your morning coffee.
You go to take a sip, and I don't stop you.

Catch 22

Mrs Callahan punctuates her name with a smiley face
and asks your class to call her Sunshine. She speaks softly.
'The project is simple,' she says, 'spend your summer
trying to catch something and prepare a presentation
about what you learned from it.' She wants to but
doesn't say, 'think outside the box.' During football
practice after class someone covers the ball with butter,
making your grasp reflex twitch with every foul ball.
They blame the twenty-seven-nil defeat on your role
as goalkeeper, so you walk home alone. You hope
that on the way you'll find a butterfly, catch the butterfly,
teach the butterfly how to play football and be your
friend and fill an entire novel with wide-shot photos
of your summer epiphany. But the sky is clear.

After your mum unplugs your nightlight you scurry
under the covers to play *Pokémon,* preparing a monologue
for class about the Gen Z generation and how things
don't need to be held to be had anymore. But no
matter how many times you stumble upon a wild Pidgey
in the tall grass, all you seem to do is make them faint.
Before you know it, July is slipping away, so you start
spending your nights hidden at the bottom of your parents'
wardrobe to, as your sister put it, 'catch them in the act.'
But their snoring just reminds you of the wind, intangible.

On the first day back your bag is empty, and as a final
act of desperation while waiting to present to the class
you lean closer to the girl in front hoping to catch headlice.
But she smells like dish soap and her summer findings are
stapled. When the teacher enters the classroom, you attempt
to crawl into yourself like a Russian nesting doll but emerge
only when she takes a permanent marker to the smart board
and writes Miss Callahan in capital letters. She speaks simply.
'From now on,' she says, 'let's just be honest with each other.
Someone's been stealing all my time and I'd like it back.
Whoever is responsible needs to place it back down on my
desk by the end of the day, and don't let me catch you again.'

Don't Adjust

You're sitting home alone watching your television
tell a story it doesn't really understand. Right now
it shows a pretty woman sitting on a leather chair
complaining about the air con. There's a man
stage left with his legs crossed and he says:
   'and how does that make you feel?'
And she says something... philosophical.
Violins begin to play distantly in the backdrop,
this means that he is smart, and she is sad.
The actress on screen is trying to remember
what nervousness looks like, unfolds her arms,
starts to scratch them. She takes an exaggerated
sip of her sparkling water, the condensation leaving
a ring on his polished mahogany as she cries:
   'my night times are the hardest.'
And suddenly it cuts to an advert about dishwasher
salt and you remember you haven't eaten in three days.
Then it cuts to black and you remember you haven't
paid the electricity bill this month. Then it starts
to rain in your living room because that's what
your TV thinks sadness looks like. Because being sad
is a beautiful woman on expensive upholstery while
you're just standing here in the rain feeling ugly.

ELEANOR BURLEIGH

Eleanor Burleigh is a poet and writer who finds inspiration in the sensory and is a fan of experimenting with language and images. She has previously had work published in *Spoonfeed* magazine and is currently based in Hampshire.

eleanorburleigh02@gmail.com

Poems
un-recognition
Monday night malnutrition
loose change
disembodiment

un-recognition

the baby in the frame is
puff-faced round-apple
cheeked suspended as if
in ice in the monochrome

smallset eyes stuffed
between skin folds gaze
out emptily is there

a hesitance in the quirk
of rightside lip is the
curling shadow on
the left of her face

flush or light redirected
the hair wisps float against
the frame cow lick
holding its own against
 plastic insert

a whitetucked collar-
shirt obscures any neck
she is a head propped
up in a smeared dirt-
dribbling frame the snail-

trail slithering up
& down the wooden
beam a puppet
string attaching

a brow slightly wonky a
front-tooth-gap pearly in
its black-mouth-mass

that's the beauty of
old photographs you
can never tell which
is grime / or skin

Monday night malnutrition

a plastic duck bobs a wet
trickle of tongue in
the bath tub

white streaked leer
with its bulbous
nasal drip

I am reading All About Love™ in
pdf format on blue Night Time™
mode on my phone

the shuddering branches
against the window
make me feel disconnected

from Love™ and Nature™
and these sausage-y eczema-
cracked fingers as they

dutifully flick from
one page
to the next

wind rattles the
blue door frame &
a floor board creaks

& my body keeps score
of an itch in an
eyelid pillowing

blood as chipped nail
dislodges scab crust
on a knee this

hunch of neck and
back spinal column
contorting as I curl in-

wards foetal thigh to
stomach embrace
nuzzling on

a new kind
of amniotic fluid

loose change

my hand outstretched is reaching for
prickly fluff mothballed among
fruit flies old tesco bags with bright
flowers lining the long drive
                  &
plastic music that drums on my tongue

nails graze pink-tin dancers along the
ceiling of a tiny room above a single
bed twisted alabaster
                &
  lumps over toes

a smell of dust coating dried cranberries
in the attic knitted-wool chin scrambling
  &
small feet tangled
jewellery round little hot fingers

there's music from a fat grey stereo
a spit & crackle of white bones
in dark fire

the smack of swirling plastic fairy light wings

& black sidling in through the window
& a hot voice simmering
& sliding wide banister chips swooshes breaks

disembodiment

a fat clock-finger grabs
my skull spidery-press of
metal licking dandruff-
spit takes me apart my
legs still in bed cool toes
sticking out

under the duvet my eyes
placed with care on the
dresser a sugar-glaze
hum of shape against
wallpaper my arms are

in june sticky with juice
sweat and cider-spit
they flab my stomach
is drifting in the sky
somewhere guts dipping

into ice cream from a
melting paper cup they
rise and dribble a sweet
creamy pink my fingers

hunch between leaf
and dirt-lip stuffed up
they could be tipped over
and excavated vein-pink throb

papery under someone else's
warm thumb my head
gaunt and oozing is on a bench
two summers ago dried tongue

lolls out scabbing cavities
infested with silverfish and
beetle-sick

HETTY CLISS

Hetty Cliss is a poet and spoken word artist from East Anglia. Her poems have been featured in Backlash Press's *Isolation Journal* and shortlisted for the Fish Publishing Lockdown Prize. Her recent work explores co-dependency, addiction, and the relationship between poetic form, the body, and the home.

hetty.cliss@gmail.com

Poems
Inhibition
Focal Point Arrhythmic
Horse Girl
First Love

Inhibition

i am always carrying / a bag for life
filled with weeds, expected recipes
the bludgeoned berries
of someone else's feelings

yes, i carry messages / from your eyes
to this pigeon-toed heart of mine
but at night words split us open
and we lick up the cut

talk carries / a wreath of lilies
but i fear what lifts in the light
like a sparkling dew or a bruise
struck green in healing

the weeds are creeping quicker
now, can't you feel them?

Focal Point Arrhythmic

when you are bad   you say bad bad   and i swoop in riding rings of denial   no   not bad bad   good bad   good bad doing the best it can   good bad dragged to doom   sinking   to the sofa in the living room   heart beating   to a count of three   b a d b a d b a d good bad unaware   as i dart downstairs   good bad climbing behind clenched eyes   searching   for self-pity's peak   so far   so high and far when you next croak   bad bad   from a spent throat   it seems too faint to mean anything even when i know   the tone of your crawling speech   good bad   still beating   b a d b a d b a d   and shrinking to screech   bad bad   hoping to reach ears   all blocked with sand   you keep me good   to set you bad but everything   is blanket grey   yes   you've been bad   again so let my goodness flit in   so healing   so ready   to tuck you in   so ready to pin you   to your actions   hammer hands caressing   bad bad bad bad   i smile and swing   smile and swing and say   no not bad bad good bad   good bad doing the best it can   blanket gripped to chin   beating beaten by sleep   so silent   and still   and good

Horse Girl

I want to revisit Virginia Woolf.
I'm pulling weeds in the garden (you are
what you eat), thinking of the time Miss Cole
gave us the answers to a Jubilee
Weakest Link class contest to learn, rather
than stacks of factsheets. My memory whetted
as I read and re-read regal stats to
parrot back in the multi-class contest.

Jack was my partner (as useful as an
appendix). I hate ragwort, but I love
Woolf. (Horses mistakenly munch weeds to
death.) I hate the grip of dirt under nails.

No one suspected I'd cheated. Many
eager and snivelling years preceded me.

First Love

    Let's not rush.
    We wait a month
    to fuck
    which means we're making love.
    Flirting
    the inherited game
    embroidered quirks
    repeat as new.
    I'm not the one
    to sponge mildew from the walls
    of your student bedroom
    but find myself sopping all the same.

                                In the Sea Life Centre
                                we watch the turtle drift
                                beneath the glass-floor boat.
                                Do you think it's lonely?
                                We laugh like it's a joke.

    The end isn't quick.
    Connection must crack
    unquenched
    before it can be demolished.
    History must be cut
    before the threaded years restitch.
    At times slow thoughts
    get caught wandering
    before memory can sift
    to comprehension. Just now
    I found myself caught alone
                            and afloat.

ABIGAIL CRAIG

Abigail Craig is a poet from Hartlepool, living in Norwich. Before her MA, she received a BA in English Literature with Creative Writing from UEA. She does her best writing by the sea, tending towards topics of place, memory and loss. Abigail has a growing preoccupation with environmentalism.

abigailcraig99@gmail.com

Poems
The Isle of Cumbrae

The Isle of Cumbrae

I

I visit my grandmother's headstone once more before departing,
feel the equalising temperatures of the pink
granite and my palm while reciting the island (this time)

to her, to an audience of open-beaked goldfinch fledglings,
to the yellow of the flowers dulled in the cathedral's shadow.
Returning is a loop in a length of thread

each poem I read aloud: a loose tracery of that crossing
and I (wanderer, paddler, mourner, recaller)
endlessly at the brink of all at once

everything and nothing at all but
persistent juvenile begging and
primrose, primrose, buttercup, broom.

II

The Isle of Eroding signs:

this is the labradorite lion ploughing the gorse,
                            remembering
how it cleaved itself from an Ice Age. Now reading as a two-sided sign:

      you have almost reached Millport / you have almost left it behind.
      Here is the disused curling pond / here is the passing slab of colder winters.
                                                                             Here
is the secret neck of a heron,
    here you are
watching it by fairy light.
      These are the ripples of its leaving / these are the ripples of your arriving.
      These are the painted teeth of The Crocodile Rock / this is the salt peeling
of them.

        That is the sound of four gannets / final echo
of the hundreds that flew from pudding island
                    all those years ago.
This (I will point to it with my smallest fingernail),
is the shape of a canine tooth on a map.
But this, (with my toes at the water-edge)
is the unhemmed cusp
of a place, signposted somewhere on the pitch tilt of a peesweep's call,
                                 someplace
between the wind torn thrift of the west,
and the sheltered asphodel of the east.

III

                             It feels as if,
at any moment, you could lower the lip of your plastic bucket
and this place would rush right into it:

shingle, bladderwrack, three hermit crabs hiding in their shells,
half a razor clam, a handful of cockles, a mermaid's purse, a portion of a wave,
a lion made of rock, the whitest gannets in the world, a fresh water spring,
the tailfins of a humpback whale tilted to the sky, the promise of keeping it all.

In the moment following, you would be left with no choice but to
upend your bucket.

IV

A sound like the scraping together of a blast and a sigh
grits my ear.
Turning, I glimpse its lectern tailfins and
tether their plateaux

to the wild orchids I take care
not to step on, the orange windsock flailing east,
the Waverley steamer at the pier,
the goldfinch fledglings I have been
watching in the cathedral graveyard.

I wonder what will become of this place;
will it find its route and swim to the Arctic
will it sink to the bottom of the Firth of Clyde

V

And in my wondering
I know nothing richer than a ten-minute rockpool.

Standing at the shore line, I remember
we were mere feet from the lowest tide;

my grandmother bent over the brink of barnacles,
delved through the surface with her hands.
Cupping, she showed me a moon jellyfish gently

flouncing itself against her palms, a little stranger,
the creases between her fingers otherworldly, magnified,
the callouses, the gold wedge of a ring.

I slid my hands under it, a strange new world
prickling slightly, saltwater on the graze of memory
before the first rush of turning,

a pulling at both ends, the hard lump of a knot,
those lilac rings disappearing into the foam.

I felt that, the leaving of it.

SAM DAVIDSON

Sam Davidson was born days after the collapse of the USSR. 23 years and a big acid trip later, he was encamped with 2,500 refugees. Discover this and other far-out experiences in *Love's Many Names* (Angelico Press). Buy it on Amazon and contribute to the free press worldwide.

srwdavidson@gmail.com

Poems
Oysters
Apples
Milk Teeth
A man is angry with me
Red spider
Sophia

Oysters

the oyster shell
before it became an object
was part of a being
thing
a living-dead
container of life
like our skein of skin

pearls they say are
grit-gotten goods
discomfort digested
and pain consumed
they lead to expressions
of pure luminescence
and piquing out
beauty from flesh
in death
they irridesce

how it feels
to be an oyster
escapes me
whether it's soft like me
or brittle like the millipede
can it feel its own rigidity
does it know its own fragility
does it hunger and languor
can it feel rage or anger
and how does it open its shell
does it loosen its hinges
to make love by inches
or all at once in a spasm of will?

whether the act of eating an oyster
shucked and squirming in lemon is sin
is beyond this song
because I cannot see whether nature or we
know right or wrong
nor whether the oysters agree

Apples

See how the ruddy apple gleams
In the shadows of our dreams
It seems to us the fruit of fates
This thing that taste and meaning mates

Eve and Adam knew its flesh
Sin was young and love was fresh
Later children learned to blame
What God left guileless of a name

Fearless Eris let it lie
Countless Greeks set out to die
Odysseus was lost at sea
And many sought Penelope

Arthur went unto his rest
Amongst the orchards of the West
Britons wait for his return
Or seek the Grail its tale to learn

We pick the apples with our hands
That glow across the autumn lands
They fruit just as the year grows old
Returning the past as gifts of gold

The spring of seed and fertile flower
Summer's growing, golden hour
Winters wait, whose fallen hoard
Will feed us with its sugars stored

Every taste is bittersweet
Wearily go the wanderer's feet
One day, they say, we'll walk anew
And taste those apples that we grew

Meanwhile, open your gardens wide
At springtime as in autumn-tide
We who rest and toil and play
Will plant by night the seeds of day

Milk Teeth

the cupboard door
has come off its hinges
it is so empty inside
that nothing has slithered out
onto the carpet
to face me

I see you there
having waited your turn
to come creeping out over
the bedroom floor

like the long furby
Sophia made
kept hidden from me
at the back of her wardrobe

she had taken apart
a sweet '90s furby
inserted a spine
elongated
and swathed in cow-print
she Frankenstein'd
back on the feet
and named him
Milk Teeth

when I saw him I said
I am yours to keep
but you must also take
the long furbys
in my wardrobe

A man is angry with me

You can tell can tell when they're angry at you
For daring to do something he
Was planning on daring to do
And ever since then he's found reasons
That show why he's right and I'm wrong
And I'm sure that he's glad beyond measure
That he never had plans all along

I'm sure when he looks in the mirror
He's proud of his will and his strength
And I'm sure that one day he'll be daring
And someone will judge him at length
There are those who cannot and will not
There are those who dare not and die
And then there are those who have reasons
To separate Earth from the Sky

Red spider

    hanging
    from a house high
    thread
    in your indoor garden
    waits
    all action
    suspended

Sophia

I see your golden strands of hair
Lit up on a bed of brown
And all my future standing there
Where you are lying down

ROSE FRANCKLIN

Rose Francklin is a mother of five children and an artist. She received her postgraduate from the Royal Academy Schools. She has worked as a teacher, gardener, and art facilitator for adults with special needs. She currently lives in Norfolk.

Poems
Stone House
Orchid
The Dressed Crab

Stone House

Light travels from room to room, as if one eye
is open, another awakes, and then
Large square eyes, staring at the dark
(never more than two or three at a time)

A bird begins to sing. The village lane shines. Cars are skimmed with ice.

And every night, a different light
tracking time, an experiment of hours.
The beast is asleep
but never completely; the great brain of security
corroded   blinking   its slow morse code

Orchid

      an arc
      a waterfall
      of pale-lime voices
      pulse of larynx   open open
      — no voice?   listen
      throats spiced   cinnamon

      untouched clarity without utterance

      to do with tongues,
              dulling grass gleans
      length of a sun bear's tongue
      three together, not altogether unharmed
         licking the air, bowing
            resolved
      whittled parchment edges
      merging into beach
      or spit of land

      above
      the unentangling:
           weaning lisps
      sprouted tentacular beneath
           tentative up-reachings
      sidling in-between
           others downward,
      a tumbled breaking greyed —

all of this grown through
              disassembling
arid footings, no adherence to earth
the simple splittings meshing together
the hidden intricacy,

the song   in months of song

The Dressed Crab

comes wrapped in the front page
of The Daily Telegraph's
Features & Arts section:
Can a royal ever truly be private?
a patterning tri-coloured package:
Di and Charles on plates, in hearts,
Kate and Will carrying
a blanketed bundle, framed on mugs
only the backs of Meghan & Harry,
only the hands of Eugenie, husband
and unnamed child
and it's all quite fetching,
unlike the normal newsprint,
and British, as if I'm carrying
a folded flag — given
to honour a hero's grave,
but mostly, it makes
the poor dressed crab seem grand.
truly be private?
this article is making it hard.
I look at the crab
all shucked and clean,
dressed to appeal,
with one triple-jointed claw,
exclamatory —
two days ago a passenger at sea,
doing its scuttling, galactic thing;
no longer anonymous,
this *Cancer pagurus*
now a rock-bed thesaurus,

and my moon is in cancer.
I put it back in the fridge

GABRIELLE GRIOT

Gabrielle Griot is a writer from Massachusetts. In her past lives, she worked as a cruise ship stewardess, a small-town journalist, a sports bar hostess, a coconut oil salesperson and a senior copywriter. She is the proud mother of several houseplants, a collection of unhinged poems and an emerging novel.

gabriellegriot@gmail.com

Poems
High Resolution
Leaving 404
Age Difference
Lately I've Been Crying
Two Truths and a Lie

High Resolution

I drink enough so it feels good
or like nothing   I can't remember

can't stop opening the orifice
the horned wound   the pulpy rotten cavity

sometimes, pretend to be dead

lie there like you're dead. doesn't matter
if you're dead   they'll do it anyway

dead girl is insatiable   she'll swallow herself
whole she'll swallow you too   she'll drink every last drop

    & say *thank you* for the privilege

I'll dissociate like one of your French philosophers
right there   in the shower   on the bed   on the floor
surrounded by wolves   licking their lips   stroking their

    until the Censor blacks it out

Leaving 404

look me in the monitor and tell me I'm here
in your tie-dye shirt drenched in ultraviolet
you can't see but I'm buffered and untethering
and I can't do it on demand but I pretend I can
because simultaneity's nice and you tell me that
you love me when you do. it was paradise really
in your supersonic home & now the Amazon
is just asphalt and dust but I guess we'll always
have the Berkshires & Laurie Anderson &
Adam Duritz & everyone who thinks this poem
is about them it's not but it's fun to pretend
I'm not split or spectral or possibly incapable
of love. take a number on your way in.
we'll call you when it's your turn.

Age Difference
The opening to a hybrid piece of poetic prose

I'm nineteen the first time a man massages my feet. Mike is thirty-five but tells me he's twenty-nine and it all feels very grown-up: boxed reds from the bodega across the street and Long Island iced teas I'm told to pretend are just plain old iced teas if anybody asks, but of course nobody does.

At the bar where we work everyone is fucking. When Mike isn't bartending he's fucking another bartender named Lexie and teaching twelfth-grade history at the local charter school. When we fuck he grips my small tits and moans that he wishes I were his student, that he'd bend me over the desk and fuck me, right there in his classroom.

I play along, naturally. I played along with almost everything in those days. Years later, a friend will remark on the way young women straddle the space between supreme power and supreme powerlessness, and I'll nod passively: sifting through the silver of memory, blacks and whites, synaptic shades of grey. At nineteen all I see is spangled, aching colour.

Lately I've Been Crying

with gratitude at the small things
like when my Experian credit report

tells me I'm exceptional
         & I almost believe it

christening new lashes with castor oil
& cradling the rice like somebody's baby

crawling up the stairs & kissing
your best friend in a dream

         things happen
         & I let them

driving perfectly straight
down American roads that go on &

on forever & ever amen
lying   perfectly straight

on latex floors lacerating
my emptiness   afterbirthing angels

in apostatic snow
        lately I just think about

pearlescent pinks
cooked   & unspooling

over me in the shower again
&   again it's a lot less effort

to close my eyes & think about
everything I've ever thought about

than actually having to try it for myself
        & besides nothing feels good

except strip mall margaritas
& rum punch by the jukebox

bookmarking our delusion
bloodletting our thirst   beneath the supermarket moon

     hey I love you
     I'm sorry about everything

Two Truths and a Lie

Joni Mitchell doesn't want to be called confessional
She thinks Anne Sexton was a dirty liar
Who couldn't even be honest with her shrink
But I don't think the point of poetry is to be honest
And I don't think the point of life is to shrink
I don't know if there's even a point to honesty
Like if I change my mind five times in an hour
That doesn't exactly make me sane
But it also doesn't make me a liar
I don't know why I said I had a process
I don't have a process
I don't even have a savings account
I don't know where I'm going to be in five weeks
Let alone five years
And I can't stop writing terrible poetry
And telling terrible lies
When another of my favourite artists gets sober
I don't think oh that's great for them
Instead I think another one bites the dust
And then I pour myself another drink
I don't believe in radical tenderness
I don't believe in unabashed joy
I don't believe in anything at all
I used to want to write beautifully
Now I just get called brave for saying fuck in all my poems
It's pathetic that I'm writing
From this meta-confessional point of view
This poem is objectively bad
And will be called out as such by the editors
But I can't stop posting cringe
On the internet of life
It's an addiction
Like irony-poisoned golf or infinite scroll
Expensively scented candles or autofictional masturbation
I'm not good at poetry
But I'm also not good at anything else

My therapist says there's nothing wrong with me
But she'll prescribe the antidepressants if I want them

ALEX HILLMAN

Alex Hillman is a poet living in Norwich. She is interested in writing about the body, consciousness, technology and gender, informed by their interest in music, anime and history, amongst others. When she's not writing, they can be found baking, playing guitar, or impulsively dyeing their hair.

Alexandra.hillman22@gmail.com

Poems
I Have Taken on the Name of Ammit
Two Thirds of the way Between Bouba and Kiki
Playboy's Roller Disco & Pajama Party (1979)

I Have Taken on the Name of Ammit

When you say a name like my name you mean DEVOURER, SOUL-EATER
but you wrap it in cartouche,
to keep it hidden. I punish in a thousand tongues
AMMIT, AMMIT, AMMIT and you rinse the blood
out of my hair and hold me
while I cry in the tub. You say my name like a name,
like DEVOURER, SOUL-EATER sounds pretty,
not like a word like that can't be taken back
when it's been spat out.
I offer it to you with bare-neck
DEVOURER, SOUL-EATER
like a naked glyph whispered into view.

You do not write a name
like a name but like a bent arm, two owls,
a loaf of bread that sound AMMIT, AMMIT, AMMIT
and I appear,
not like a name like AMMIT,
but as a hippopotamus, lion,
crocodile, like a DEVOURER, SOUL-EATER.
I have eaten many heavy hearts
that were unworthy like a monster,
like a thing like AMMIT, but you touch gently

like a body that is not mine

like the second owl that means death

like a soul I can't eat.

Two Thirds of the way Between Bouba and Kiki

01010100 01110111 01101111 00100000 01010100 01101000 01101001
01110010 01100100 01110011 00100000 01101111 01100110 00100000
01110100 01101000 01100101 00100000 01110111 01100001 01111001
00100000 01000010 01100101 01110100 01110111 01100101 01100101
01101110 00100000 01000010 01101111 01110101 01100010 01100001
00100000 01100001 01101110 01100100 00100000 01001011 01101001
01101011 01101001 00001010 00001010 01000001 01101100 01101100
00100000 01110100 01101000 01100101 00100000 01101110 01100101
01110111 00100000 01001110 01100101 01110111 00100000 01000001
01100111 01100101 01110010 01110011 00001010 01101000 01100001
01110110 01100101 00100000 01110111 01101111 01110010 01100100
01110011 00100000 01100110 01101111 01110010 00100000 01110100
01101000 01101001 01101110 01100111 01110011 00001010 01100010
01110101 01110100 00100000 01001001 00100000 01100011 01100001
01101100 01101100 00100000 01101101 01111001 01110011 01100101
01101100 01100110 00100000 01100011 01101111 01101100 01101111
01110101 01110010 01110011 00100000 01100001 01101110 01100100
00100000 01110011 01101000 01100001 01110000 01100101 01110011
00100000 00001010 01100010 01101100 01110101 01110010 01110000
01101100 01100101 00101100 00100000 01100010 01101111 01110101
01100010 01100001 00100000 01100001 01101110 01100100 00100000
01101011 01101001 01101011 01101001 00001010 01101111 01110010
00100000 01101110 01100101 01101001 01110100 01101000 01100101
01110010 00101100 00100000 01110111 01101000 01100001 01110100
01100101 01110110 01100101 01110010 00100000 01101100 01101001
01100101 01110011 00100000 01100010 01100101 01110100 01110111
01100101 01100101 01101110 00101110 00001010 01010000 01100101
01110010 01101000 01100001 01110000 01110011 00100000 01110111
01101000 01100101 01101110 00100000 01101101 01111001 00100000
01100011 01101111 01101110 01110011 01100011 01101001 01101111
01110101 01110011 01101110 01100101 01110011 01110011 00001010
01101001 01110011 00100000 01110101 01110000 01101100 01101111
01100001 01100100 01100101 01100100 00100000 01110100 01101111
00100000 01110100 01101000 01100101 00100000 01110011 01111001
01110011 01110100 01100101 01101101 00001010 01100001 01101110
01100100 00100000 01001001 00100000 01100011 01100001 01101110

00100000 01100100 01101001 01110100 01100011 01101000 00100000 01110100 01101000 01101001 01110011 00100000 01100010 01101111 01100100 01111001 00001010 01001001 11100010 10000000 10011001 01101100 01101100 00100000 01100011 01101000 01101111 01101111 01110011 01100101 00100000 01110100 01101111 00100000 01110011 01110100 01100001 01111001 00100000 01101111 01101110 01101100 01101001 01101110 01100101 00100000 01110111 01101001 01110100 01101000 01101111 01110101 01110100 00100000 01101111 01101110 01100101 00001010 01100001 01101110 01100100 00100000 01101000 01101111 01110110 01100101 01110010 00100000 01101001 01101110 00100000 01101110 01101111 00100000 01100100 01101001 01101101 01100101 01101110 01110011 01101001 01101111 01101110 01110011 00100000 01100001 01110100 00100000 01100001 01101100 01101100 00111010 00001010 Non Binary Code.

(translation on next page)

Two Thirds of the way Between Bouba and Kiki

All the new New Agers
have words for things
but I call myself colours and shapes
blurple, bouba and kiki
or neither, whatever lies between.
Perhaps when my consciousness
is uploaded to the system
and I can ditch this body
I'll choose to stay online without one
and hover in no dimensions at all:
01001110 01101111 01101110 00101101 01000010 01101001 01101110
01100001 01110010 01111001 00100000 01000011 01101111 01100100
01100101.

Playboy's Roller Disco & Pajama Party (1979)
For Dorothy Stratten

They turned the tennis court into a roller rink;
itsy bitsy shorts and champagne from a fountain. Play pool
by the pool and don't stop laughing,
whatever you do. Heff's got a babe
 for each day of the week –
remember when we threw him his own Olympics?
– and says Tuesday like 'two's day'. Anyway, Dorothy,
what an afternoon it was, mimosas,
and the sky was just as orange.

Dorothy, playing games with the reporter,
smiling at celebrities if Paul would let you,
and we all wished our hair would fluff like yours.
Bikinis and trumpets and the Village People.
The gents liked you best.
Here in the mansion
it's a roller disco and pajama party
every day.

Playmate of the year 1980
and it was the happiest you said you'd been
until Paul sold your car for cash.
We thought it was bad then, Dorothy,
we wanted to keep you safe;
film doesn't fade when you lock it in the dark.
Two years and one day since you arrived in L.A.
and they all wanted to own you
(and we did too, Dorothy).

Hollywood called our names, and we were dumb
enough to listen, that's what leaves you twenty on screen forever,
that's what gets your tits on print.
Baby, you got star potential,
your death will make a man out of a moron
and a bunny of a girl, Dorothy,
and we cried
and Peter cried
and then he married your sister.

MAYA HOUGH

Maya Hough is a lifelong writer and poet from Nottinghamshire, who has been living and studying in Norwich since 2016. Morbid yet retaining a sense of humour, her work definitely reflects her personality and her experience in life as a young woman. Find her on Twitter (@maya_hough) or Instagram (@mayahoughpoetry).

maya.j.hough@gmail.com

Poems
Throw me back to sea
Online Horoscopes
Woman/Debris
Girlhood
'When will we feel each other's touch again?'

Throw me back to sea

I don't think I knew your love,
just your knife, your mouth:

                              Gut me,
                         I will bleed out
                    like a fish in your hands.

Online Horoscopes

      apparently I'm ruled by Venus
      a Taurus   stubborn with her
      mouth   stuffed   full
      of cyclical argument and

            I watch mystics on TV
      talk to ghosts   I watch Anthony Bourdain
      think of   killing myself
      for some conversation

      One time I drew   The Tower
         unknowingly and
      my roommate   comatosed
         had her heart cut open

      unknowingly I drew The Tower
         for myself   inked out the deck
        haunted   by cardboard
      cleansed   with crystals

      My ascendant sign is also
      the name of an   experimental
      film about gay men   and Nazis
      icon worship   motorbikes

      my mind   always wanders
      back to Anthony Bourdain
      Miami foodscapes   and
         eating my words

Woman/Debris

        no longer 'body'
        washed ashore the beach and
        pulled to land by your disaster

        My, what strong hands you have!

        I have sirenned myself and
        destroyed such wanting men, yet
        your undesperate touch is what
        finally dragged me under.

Girlhood

I.
A beach in Scotland,
frozen sand and
clear water,
grab the boat
or take a dip
to feel the cold
and numb the ache.

II.
The fly rams its body
repeatedly
against the glass.
It can see the garden
but not the
open window
20cm away.

III.
The feathers on the doorstep
have a history
and a corpse,
but the cat's stomach
is full and you think about
her face on the news
and men's whiskers.

IV.
A beach in Scotland,
frozen sand and
frozen water,
jump the boat
and take a dip,
the cold can't
outweigh the ache.

V.
The fly rams its body
against the glass The fly
rams its body against the
glass The fly rams its
body against the glass The
fly rams its body against the
glass The fly rams its

'When will we feel each other's touch again?'

        white letters
        scrawled to catch our eyes,
        but still we peer
                over the edge
                of the concrete overpass,

        chain-linked fingers and metal
        (I used to feel so caged here.)

        They must make paint specially
        for sentiments,
                to cover
            vulnerability, strip it away
            from the public eye.

        I guess we cross the bridge, and
        just forget nice thoughts
                for now.

P B HUGHES

P B Hughes's poems have appeared in the *New Statesman*, *The Rialto*, *Magma Poetry* and *Lighthouse*. Her pamphlet, *Girl, falling*, was published in September 2019 by Gatehouse Press. She was shortlisted for the 2017 Bridport Poetry Prize and the 2019 Fish Poetry Prize. She lives in London and is working on a full-length collection.

pennybhughes@gmail.com

Poems
everything got a bit
earth song
The Undertaking
dream sequence
Mother's Day
The End of Poetry

everything got a bit

& not the way beginnings would begin there were no ribbons
no fanfares lights
did not dim no parting of curtains governments rolled
off our tongues the moon swerved a star mars
built its first restaurant
                                    we ate mouthfuls of ego mouthfuls of blue
blew bubbles from a gum
of language volcanoes ashed into city
centres dead fish
swelled harbours there was no
rain for a season leaves tore strips of the sky
to chew on & when someone called the operator to ask what
was happening there was no dial tone
                                          snowdrops came up daffodils
a rainbow recordings of the earth
shouting went viral together we sang crows ran all news
platforms some words
took the dictionary to court & won

earth song

a person buying lottery tickets in a newsagent
a person reading a poem on the underground
a person peeling oranges for magazine shoot
a person putting dog poo in a doggie poo bag
a person rating a call with customer services
a person taking photographs of a statue
a person making a right-hand turn at a roundabout
a person scanning hand baggage at airport security
a person teaching internet safety to school children
a person watching a series about endangered animals
a person leaning out of a window in a high-rise
a person monitoring a person in an intensive care unit
a person studying models to predict climate patterns
a person using a blown-out umbrella to shelter from the sun

The Undertaking

We stoop
                        above
          the riverbank on a slant of grass rewilding
                                            children,
putting them back
        into the earth
                              and each other

the way we heard people wrap
                        apples in newspaper

      to make them last

Grassland

          full of movement like information like children are places
              to hide
                    as well as to be
                                  found

The children seed
       under trees,
                  a couple climbing shake branches into whoops

of joy at the tilt of plough
              root and soil
                            still swollen
     from a long winter

We are changed
       dizzy from talk
                      from the steep
                                  descent
   of grass,
airborne songs and this very
                      greening,

dream sequence

we are dreaming more
& more vividly a study shows & in the frenzied nights
that follow our narratives go all meta
on us. we dream we wake in a hotel room certain
we did not go to sleep there. as if
needing proof
we do & don't we dream the real sequence of events
book water teeth etc
before we went to bed. we dream
in an unknown language
of a global quest by computer programmes
to find a translation. we post
     are all dreams this deep?
it takes ages to get past heaven's
switchboard. jung claims not to have heard
about the study. not much point reading the news
when you're dead. those dreams are trying
to tell you something he says
sounding bored. are they
poems? jung could ask one of his friends. he cuts
us off. tired we dream
some more but the poem hasn't got any lines
left in it.

the poem is bored. it smoked
too many cigarettes when it was being written
was only anthologised once
& has watched the whole of netflix.
one more thing. it's really come to
    hate line six
the poem wants an alter ego which has fun
& frenzied dreams. nights are rows a
to g of empty seats in a cinema
currently not showing.
it attends a local dream test centre & scores
a negative. on the way home it calls

the association of counselling & psychotherapy
whose receptionist recommends a course
in conscious unconsciousness
but it's twenty weeks. instead
the poem leaves messages
for all the descendants of freud
asking for pointers. the freud who works in media
calls back. if any interesting
dreams come up he'll send out
a press release. the poem dreams it wins
a competition which pays for an overseas
trip. birds waterfalls forests beaches
even the sea is computer generated. in the dream
the poem sits on a bench by a temple
phones the tourist board & is put
on hold. the dream carries on
but the narrative
stops. there's no way out. the poem is stuck
inside the dream.

the poem wakes & wants a rewrite but we're dreamers
not poets it's our way of coping
with life. what
not even a rethink of line six?
we dream less or
our targeted memory reactivation
is affected. we order a dream catcher
which is out of character
& dream a national no
fancy dress policy. we're at a party
in normal outfits & everyone's wearing animal
costumes. we don't understand
what they're saying
& the party gets busted
by police. we dream we are sitting on a runway
in a boeing seven four seven which can't take off
because the sky has turned to jelly
blue as e number one hundred & thirty three.
we want to talk to god

about this but our phone has been infected
with a virus
     in real life
it seems & is posting pictures of the poem's holiday
in which the poem looks like an actual
person & everyone thinks it's us
& we think shit
maybe it is.

Mother's Day

Instead my daughter has been creative
      with staples, four teased into circles
clipped to her nose
lower lip and earlobes, audacious
as the day I brought her home
from hospital, set her brisk limbs on a hill
of bedcover and breathed her slight
animal smell back into me. Hours
      played us like counters and when daylight
came the walls ached with her newness. What
if the walls will mark this day as every
other, equal and less ordinary
than the last? Every day, every
      new presence is contradictory. I won't
think of her first
misspelled card, paper tissue glued as flowers

The End of Poetry
For Ada Limón

Tell me it's not and anyway, you can't
be serious. Blasphemy is ordinary as any hour
but still. Calling for it not to call for it is a kind
of logic. Knee deep in river I have fallen out of faith
with god, panning days for gold, I'm done with words
I keep in jars. Cardamon, cinnamon, star anise,
vanilla pod. Talking of stars—dead for epochs
by the time they scattergun the sky—yes, I, too
am done with the lapse between a living thing
and its perception, done with day as an acquaintance,
life as metaphor. Tell me poetry is a living
thing. Give me a better metaphor for life
than living. I'm through with the ache of armchairs,
sharp light and tired clouds, over the assault
of feet, blood and all the names for colour, over
an attachment to the smell of books, how in hands
they come alive but won't return touch. Alone on a bus
I long to gently use my arms only there's a sign:
Do not speak to or distract the driver. To carry on
or not to carry on, to ball this body tight
before I go to sleep, distanced from it in the morning
by the call of birds, the empty street, I'm over it all.
Yet isn't poetry action more than act—
a verb, a text that ripples through the spinal cord?

ELKE HUISMANS

Elke Huismans lives in Norwich, works in Cambridge and tries not to write poems about being on trains.

elke.huismans@gmail.com

Poems
Hegel's Plant Woman
Psycho-Astronomy
The None
We Live

Hegel's Plant Woman

Stand in woods. Wait
to know what it means.

An early moon is caught
in geometric branches;
8 leaves fall.

In spring, there was a red rosette
tied to a shrub; a single, white tennis shoe;
then small green buds tinged with pink.

No vivid equations
determine this moment, yet

10 leaves fall;
the moon is released.

Psycho-Astronomy

Contentions:
(I)

    The moon is debris
    made pearl

    The moon is a dearth
    clothed in visual excess

    Space autumn
    Celestial Venice

(II)

    We are ripples in bodies —
    our particle state

    Fixed in place
    when observed by ourselves:

    I've become The Philosopher at the long parties
    You see, all that is gone echoes on

    (like light)

The None

A woman has an awkwardly shaped lump of fluctuating mass, kept
     like a vow

It's impossible to say where it ends but it starts in her and she believes
     it's hollow

To own such an absence is excessive. She wants to tell, like fishermen,
but can't stretch
     far enough

Ice
     does not describe its crevasse

Sometimes, she can almost contain it, like embracing the sound of a
bell:
     here   or there
     deep   or round

When it presses in her, she wants to press back, take a bite, dip her
tongue in,
     see what comes out

No need to fear

We live

in unchartered territory	we know so little about	how to survive	without shelter
cynicism	is a lousy defence	when you're drowning	in terrifying
newsfeeds	or a wrecking ball of hogwash with no content	it's an outrageous, undemocratic	howl of pain
horrifying and loathsome	or a mirror-image calamity	of ourselves	fears rise
and there is a sharp decline in coherence	on such important issues we are clueless	economic damage or political damage	escalating violence
or complete environmental breakdown	never mind a sense of shared humanity	it's upsetting to be called 'complicit'	or
what have we done?	the objective is to avoid being dragged	under	when our
agency amounted to sweet fuck all	protest	strike	petition
vote	or the least useless option	no hyperbole	we have very limited options
and no prospect of a safety net	go for a walk with me	towards horror	or wait it out

(Twitter Collage 25/10/2019)

ALEX INNOCENT

Alex Innocent is from Yorkshire but chooses to live in East Anglia. She was the 2020/21 recipient of The Bryan Heiser Memorial Bursary.

alexinnocent@innocent.com

Poems
Alarm
Dth
The Cleansing
Birding
Therapist, dear

Alarm

> One of the greatest ways to start the day
> is with Pepsi Cola. It may be last night's
> shadow sipped straight from the can, so avoid
> slipped nicotine stumps and any ants.
>   The cigarette,
> too, is one of the best ways to start the day. It should rip
> as you inhale, while your carpaccioed lungs
> turn to petrified coral.
>   A better pick-me-up
> after a tricky night is an al fresco fuck
> with a newcomer. Toilet cubicles present
> a convenient closet for this, but the bush,
> the tree – even the phone box – offer superior
> substitutes.
>   Where the day
> is gravely important: kick it off with cocaine.
> You'll oust the fog of sleep, warm the body,
> and evacuate the bowels:
> frog eaten; the day's admin begun.
>   Alternatively,
> stick with the routine standard
> and embrace these fresh hours with alcohol.
> It will creep like shy fire
> and snap as it thaws,
> a kettle on a frozen windscreen.
> The glass may crack:
>   that is how you know it's life.

Dth

Christ comes to the door.
Come in, I tell Him.
Make Yourself at home.

Save all that Proper-Pronouning
for The Father, he tells me.
My role is more fraternal.
His hands and feet
are so much smaller than I knew.

Christ drinks. He *drinks*.

Would you like a glass of water? I ask him.
You'll dehydrate.
Christ laughs.
The silver in his hair
is a repair on a well-fingered doll.
He sticks his tongue out slightly
when he makes the alveolar stop:
d. *Dth*, he says,
swirling his glass
fast in the claw of his hand.
He makes a little whirlpool in his wine.

I sense that Christ has more to say.
He doesn't stop.

The Holy Spirit comes to the door.
She shakes leaves out of the hood of her coat,
and says: is Christ here?
Come through, I tell her.
Christ has just arrived.

Christ talks, his black eyes fixed on the tablecloth.
Your English is pristine, I tell him, and he looks up.
The Holy Spirit speaks now.

You're comprehending Tongues,
she says, nodding.

But I don't understand.

My sister rings, although I have her phone upstairs.
Christ is here, I tell her.
What did you find out? she asks.
Is he a prophet?
Or is he just a fraud?

I like a lot of what he's saying, I tell her.
He wants to help the poor and sort out sin.
That's fine, she says, but is he the Son of God?
I'm not so sure on all the supernatural stuff, I tell her.
I don't even ask myself how she can speak again.

The Holy Spirit's listening and she coughs.
I'll get my coat, she says, eyebrows raised.
Come on, O Great Orator, she coos to Christ.
God's expecting us.

And then they leave my house.
There's just the empty glass,
the pile of leaves,
the ghostly warmth on the chair.

My sister calls again,
even though three years have passed since the wake.
It's the funniest thing, she says, this door.

The Cleansing

Again, they demonstrate the power
washer, shooting
the scales from a cloud-eyed fish.

But, I wonder, why stop
there? Why not trap
a cat and skin
it smartly? What about next door's
noisy dog? Imagine
this: instead of interring
grandad, we plop
him on the communal patio outside
his sheltered room, and layer
by layer, disrobe him of life's
false ornaments.
His cardigan; slippers.
Elasticated slacks
and anorak.
Next; the vague grey
of his vest and sagging
pants, blown into scraps; later hoisted
on the low, complicated
bush's branch. Let's see how soft
those vulnerable parts
can really be: eyes turned to fondant;
nipples, flying brittle
-blossom, black
seed-pods spun
into chocolate coins.
How much mousse
still encases the cherished fruit
within the aged walnut whip?
Will grandad's stuff peel
obediently, like the moulting
eczema crust
of God's russet
portcullis? Will it flake in fronds –
tender slow-roast
pork, or demand to be ripped
from sweating
poultry bones
heaped inside the whitewaxed
walls of a bargain
bucket? How far can we blast
grandad's secret offal,
strings of sausages raw,
nestling together
beneath opaque plastic tissue?
Can we hang strawberry
laces from boughs,
remnants
of silly-string on January the second?
How long before his skeleton
blooms with Hallowe'en's
beryl sherbet?
We could clean up again.
Far more gratifying to show off our power
even over such scant remains.

Birding

While I am naked in the garden
I am reminded of the video I saw

of a woman with no trousers.
She is in a car park

surrounded by sentinel vehicles
and unplugged men.

And each of these men
has something in his hand

except for one player.
He has something on his fingers.

All legs are bowed;
mounting invisible horses

in a car park, surrounded by trees
like a woodland stage.

And though there is dialogue
the birds have more urgent ideas:

louder and louder they chime
conducting the players

drowning the urges
to pound; grind; suck; come.

My local crew direct me, now,
to *just go back indoors.*

Therapist, dear

It's been so sweet: the way that you've fingered
my brain, slowly feeling your way in, wiggling
that tip with skill to stimulate something hidden.
I have loved the way you braced your forearm

over my eyes, slamming me into the corner
and screwing into the tight nugget
of real history, until it bursts open
in an arching rainbow spray of truth.

I can still feel you licking round
those hidden formative hours,
working them free, on a textbook basis.
You have exhausted me.

I look forward to our motionless embrace
and your invoice.

LAUREN KANIA

Lauren Kania is a graduate student on the poetry track at UEA. She has had poems published in *Girls Right the World*, *The South Florida Poetry Journal*, *Voice of Eve*, and the *Eckerd Review*. Whenever she isn't writing, she loves to spend time tending to her army of plants.

laurenmkania@gmail.com

Poems
My Mother, the Nymph
33687 Lee Rd, Sedalia, Missouri 65301
Grandma's Kitchen
Naperville, Illinois

My Mother, the Nymph

My mother smells of White Shoulders and Missouri musk
and has knees that seems to lose their weariness
when rooted in mud.
The only time I see her immersed in breath
is when she sinks her palms so far beneath the dirt that
her elbows smell of silt and calcium for days.

She buried my grandpa's wood-carved pipe
in red handkerchief and planted it with
the purple milkweed seeds, waiting for
molting butterflies to come and feast.

Maybe it's the snapweed she grows
or the oakmoss she walks on like carpet
or the benzoin that sits like paste on her knuckles
but I have never doubted that her bones were carved from
damp earth and cherry pits.

33687 Lee Rd, Sedalia, Missouri 65301

Missouri autumns are hard on my feet.
Cow teeth, strewn from their temporary skull,
embed in my soles and reopen the calloused skin.
I dare not rip them out or else I'll choke
on my grandpa's pipe smoke breath
as he sews the flesh back together,
his fingers that of a chemist. So I continue to
break the necks of fallen branches and hang
my toes just above the pond's edge, where catfish
threaten to bite. And when their hungry mouths
make coneflower ringlets, I bend down
as if to kiss them, one by one.

To be loved by Missouri prairies
is a different kind of love.
It tears at your ankles and eats at
the blushed tips of your ears.

I plunge my cracked nail beds deep into the dirt,
and feel what it'll be like to be buried with the cow bones.

Grandma's Kitchen

So badly do I want to feel the flame
tickle the back of my molars
as I swallow the cranberry candle wax
melting at the pinewood table
of my grandma's kitchen.

I want to taste the embers
of the carving knife used to dissect
midnight midwest beasts
and feel the farm-worn knuckles of my grandfather
cracking the clavicle of the Thanksgiving turkey.

I want that lingering shiver
of overrun ladybug legs
treading along tablecloth
feasting on fallen persimmon piths.

I want to be rooted in place
by the shag carpet's
tangled fingertips.

Naperville, Illinois

Cicada shells and crab apple cores gathered
in hands slick from the airless summer rain.
Carefully dropped into Mom's best mixing bowl
and chanted upon in a language only known by
twelve-year-old witches

Callous rain ruins the soft crunch
of freckled red leaves.
They stick to the soles of sneakers
and make the long trek from the doorstep
to the school bus
past the snapdragons
and home again

After the marigolds have wilted,
I help my grandmother blanket the
horses
bring the calves to the warm milk of their
mother's icy teats
throw the final feast of pellets to the fat
and mouthy catfish

So tempting are the crisp leaves of
The Great White Cherry Tree,
that I store the ones that have fallen
into the deepest portion of my school pockets
and sprinkle them into my water at
dinnertime, in hopes that it tastes like
April rain and checkered lily stems

VIV KEMP

Viv Kemp is a writer from Dublin, Ireland. They studied English Literature at Trinity College Dublin and hold a Master of Philosophy degree from the University of Cambridge. They edited *Icarus Magazine*, have had their work published in *Notes*, *Headstuff*, and performed at *UEA Live: New Writing*. They live in Cambridge.

versekemp@gmail.com

Poems
Robert Emmet Sonnet
Grinder
Playing *Red Dead* in Lockdown
The Mice
Flying Ants
Sherds, Unsortable

Robert Emmet Sonnet

What are you to me? X times Great Great Uncle, yes,
and a surname carried by my English Grandmother.
Your unwritten epitaph, as ordered at the dock
till, quote, 'my country takes her place among the nations
of the earth', persists as a constant, distant call,
any 'obscurity and peace' dismissed each history.
And the death, hung then beheaded, lively eyes stuck still
in a small head like a stone, the remains unclaimed, perhaps
even quartered. A Prod martyred and dashed for Catholics,
strange post-Independence; your scattered descendants later
converted in Manhattan. You live as a flat side-profile
but the gap ruptures shut when I see the Blue fly the Jack
and the slap of cleaver through corpse echoes forth and back.

Grinder
A Golden Shovel After Paul Muldoon

After the one blade all over, my head was a mink-
soft and fingers stimmed my nape as if I had escaped from
some manacle. Rebel urges squeaked like a mink-farm
in chorus and mid-class we agreed to run our own lock-in.
Cal got liquor then told us to meet in woods to the park's south.
He, whose parents bought him fireworks from Armagh, is
one we considered blessed, landlord of our illegal pub that led
us hormonal nerds to sing odes to the grave of
heroes I hadn't heard of. Later, Cal called me a Robert Nairac-
like grinder, a dork. I left with someone without saying goodbye
before hands slipped in under my shirt and teased at the fur-lined
armpits I had. We smiled and came closer, making a hood
of our hair to stay dry as we kissed. Still ashamed of his
taunts, I hid at the front of History in an anorak.

Playing *Red Dead* in Lockdown

Thank you, game, for giving me an empty world with so much
to do – acres of mountain paths and peaks that my fake horse
can trot through; stretching valleys of foxglove, lavender,
all wild and made of pixels. Thank you, coders, who crunched
eighteen-hour days. I pay tribute by staying awake
till 5AM playing your opus barely blinking,
my heartrate so high my fitbit thinks I'm swimming. Thank
you for the twenty-year friend I've just been introduced to –
I'm too depressed to message back people but Dutch tells me
to believe and sends me out for cigarettes. Thank you, game,
for making mass death more regular. My iron sights
moved honey smooth between the eyes of fifteen villagers,
the town stayed unchanged, the dead replaced like spices in a
spice rack. Thank you, game, for when I drop things it echoes.

The Mice

These traps are meant to be reusable, bought in a panic
at the tawny droppings spread out across the sofa
& dark shits clustered by the fridge. Now it's done, I hesitate
to lift the spring holding the impressed corpse together.
Burial is release into a bin, peanut butter
bait & viscera rinsed off until there's another,
but this device has pinned you whole – it should be your coffin.
We share similarities: nocturnal sallies for food
& living in a house the owners don't want you in, though
we differ on the constant stream of disease-riddled piss.
Still, I attempt amends, peeling back the trap's hammer arm
and floating you onto kitchen towel, splayed limbs stiff
& fluttering like a leaf, the feet a human pink. Then,
I look into your eye's pitch, name you, and fold the sheet.

Flying Ants

The same life cycle as fireflies
but none of the romance.
How, dull and dark, your bodies mirror
their journey's fated end.
What beauty could you possess?
Wings starched like a collar
and veined as stained glass, languidly you
blot the door frame and jamb.
Shielded with a torn-off quarter
of kitchen towel, my thumb
drives your body to pop then pinch
in scrunched-up paper, binned
thus laid to rest. Last Sunday, your buzz
and whirl scared my partner,
the old telly static of your
antic swarm making it seem
the tiles are moving! Rollicking
as a mass, flickering
body of onyx and quartz
bonded through nuptial flight
so high it trips the Met's sensor;
all this thriving to continue
life. Solid diffuse star of alates,
how wrong you have made me.

Sherds, Unsortable
For Annie

On some settlement
        an exact millennia ago,
                your body was burnt
to fine black
        particles and scooped into
                an urn for burial.
Flame can't reduce it all,
        so chalky bone parts persist
                in the dust you've become.
Someone you'll have known
        was buried whole in their bed,
                ad hoc four posters added
to lower them in
        as they lay under wool blankets
                at rest, dirt thrown on top
for a warmer covering.
        Your body knew the very limit
                of heat, stacked on a pyre
and watched by your family
        with the care that grief
                can give. Sometime
after, your body pot
        was dug up in a college
                cricket pitch and stuck
in some museum's archive stacks,
        another trophy added
                to a hidden cabinet.
In a 2000 audit,
        an assistant opened up
                the work of Victorians
and noted your shape
        disfigured and flattened
                by centuries of earth and geology.

When a pot breaks, its scattered parts are called   'sherds', not 'shards'.
The widest part is its 'shoulders', all above that,   'the neck'.
As opposed to the local noble's bed-set burial,
who was discovered as bones with veil clips
having sunk into her jaw and skeleton,
the slip from this life fell you into new form and body.
Like ages-late coroners, museum staff
anatomise and Adam at you with names,
    listing your feet,   lips,   waisted shape, bases,
          bungholes,   and knobs;   even your handles
get   labelled   as   'lugs'.

                  However, mistakes are made.
                              The still-fresh millennium
registers skull fragments
          as errant parts
                    of the urn.

There is something ill in this transformation,
          an illusion fracturing the passage given
by the old commemoration.
          Now death and science have framed you
as an object, 'detached but present',
          unsure of how they fit with the pot.
Little to love in that;
          think of a low-dug grave bearing finger bones reaching out
like roots,   or the grinding up
          of preserved Egyptian courtiers to make
                the 'Mummy Brown' pigment.

Your life was rendered
                        into unfact, an old presence
                                              now something placed
into a box marked
                'Anglo Saxon
                                Sherds,
                                              Unsortable'.

    A correction was made this year,

    a new assistant seeing

    what's left of you as not a broken

    clay piece. A quiet gift,

    separated out from the sherds

    and put in a crystal box

    for the store-based cemetery.

A second birth by way of re-classification,

a vacant, slow, two decade labour,

to acknowledge, and remember,

        you're dead,

                and had died,

                              but once   lived.

PRERANA KUMAR

Prerana Kumar is an Indian poet doing her MA in Creative Writing at UEA. An alumna of The Writing Squad, and The Writing Room 2021, she has been published in English Heritage's *'Untold Stories'*, Verve Poetry Press's *Community* and *Diversity* Anthologies, BBC's *Use Words First*, *Inkwell*, and *Ink Sweat & Tears*.

preranapkumar@gmail.com

Poems
Family Portrait as Four Nights of Diwali
Patriotic Qawwali in the Air at the Indo-Pak Border
On Hearing Arsonists Can Be Identified by Their Muslim Clothes, 2019

Family Portrait as Four Nights of Diwali

i. first night for cleanliness

we whittle rangoli made from dyed rice into the skin
of everyday, plead our living into another year. powder-spirals
net across the living room floor, cradle our caverns of laughter
crushed into the ravines cleaving the floorboards. we twirl
while we unchain our howling, still twirling while the men
say *you are the light of our homes* and mistake our brightly
draped bodies for lanterns. hoist us by our bangled arms
but not before scouring us clean of their fen-soaked fingers and
scraping our throats for their seeded sweetbrier, an unclogging
so we can sing virgin's ragas to gods and the neighbours hear
our clean flailing. in the bulbul's hour, mama breaks the bangles
hooking her upright. she pounces on the diya at the foot of his bed,
chokes it with red glass, watches the guardian flame douse.
she cackles as his stilted snores stop soiling the darkness.

ii. second night for naraka liberation

papa worships for his farmer father's peace. died
of liver failure, something to do with an excess of spirit.
at midnight, his sister's twin daughters wake, the raucous
murk of his prayers in their ears. they darken the diyas
that light the stairs outside the afterlife, cut the worship
garlands open to break the cycle of papa's forgetting.
the sickle that raked his mother's back, the kumkum
eyes that meant moonshine breath, the plough that dove
through his sister's lips and came back with the frayed strings
of her fruit, still raw and pulpy to the touch. he only
remembers how the table was set plentiful and the fruit
was fibrous in its infancy. forgets how in the hot summers
when his sister limped with her legs apart, bringing him sliced
salted mangoes, he never thought to check for her dressings.

iii. third night for the darkness

he straps me into the car seat before mama's cackles
stagger down my throat, before i digest the bitter gourd
she fattened from his hair and souped to gouge his secret.
he drives me to the towering painted narkasurs, hay men
with goat-blood veins on their weaponed arms. scimitar-
teeth casing the sins of men who worship the wealth
goddess by light to chaff her limbs apart by dark. i watch
him sear its loins with an olived torch, juice its softest
parts. his hands trace how steadily he knows a body's
ashing. his eyes glint as he places festive laddoos near
my strapped arms. watches me pinch the sugary flesh,
close-smiling how *bad men burn, you can always
tell from the teeth*. my tongue bitters with mama's gourd
and how he forgets to hide his daggers when he laughs.

iv. fourth night as kanjirottu yakshi

mama, i water my paala tree every dawn. he thinks his white island
will shield him and is reckless in the gloam. so i quench. my wrists
are ringed with scraps of sita's last saree, red with rangoli and guts,
that i stole from the bins in their driveway. my anklets are studded
with bitter-gourd seeds so i goodwill stubborn life in their gardens
before i source their men. it's just that the loneliness ghosts my diyas.
behind the tree are the last heirlooms i left with, a night full of dead
and nothing to shine for them. the camphored flesh from his thighs
is what coaxes their flicker. sometimes, i hang from the high branch
by my bangles and giggle as i remember you. you'd love how i have
no mirror and in this way i am unadorned and so unclaimed and so
i remind him of all the spoils he pillaged. before i open. looking into
that double dozen ribbed cavern, he sees where his plucked teeth sit
and why they could never name any of the remains.

Patriotic Qawwali in the Air at the Indo-Pak Border

chai	falling, stained lips vowelled through familiar
night,	thick with earthy heart,
bodies'	birth chords, snaking, unbordered
love	a line loose in raag, a slithering braid of
couplet,	echo in holy clap of palms, folded in it –
cradle	a bursting motherland
hymn	yet to spread for its twins

On Hearing Arsonists Can Be Identified by Their Muslim Clothes, 2019

Firemouth, I cannot warn your tar-flecked palms, the beginning
of the embers are already blooming their smoke-fingers

far into your lungs. I imagine your pockets are lined with family
offerings; stray lentils, a wad of gum, abbu's watch

with its minute hand standing to attention behind a cracked case,
ammi's thimble waiting to receive it. I almost say let us be wild

and hold hands, but your ears riot with the policeman's stomp
stamp howling, your coal-and-chalk striped T-shirt a running

ticker tape against the city's violet ash. Miles away,
middle-aged men lure life into their bodies

with the morning revolt of tightening a blue belt across white;
no loud unveiling, no clarion sentence, no darkmark

by which khaki-stained dog trainers single you out from the rubble.
Here, you thumb the lentils in your pocket and open throat

to their stomp stamp ascent. Palms lift, offering ammi's praise,
desperate search for a lost smoke-god your one Firemouth

with its one   name,

and how for this lotus sky it is always the same name
and how for this waiting lotus sky

not that moment yet: your veins opened like smooth
rouge lotion in your palms, your tongue cold all old iron,

your mouth a gurgling laugh. Here,
here even in your spilling smile.

SAM NEWCOMBE

Sam Newcombe joined the Poetry MA straight out of studying Creative Writing at the University of Essex. Having started as a comic prose writer, he shifted towards poetry in 2018 while studying in Passau, Germany. He is currently working towards a PGDE with Teach First.

sam.newcombe98@gmail.com

Poems
Since Watching Yuri Grieve
Opalise / Settle
Yellow
On The Day You Were Born
Yoked Cattle, One a Sojourner
The Folly

Since Watching Yuri Grieve

It just feels right
Since watching Yuri Grieve
    as a boy
To claim death and rush to acceptance
    by standing on a grave,
To do so, flowers in hand
    so that the palm remembers
    that this is about love,
And then to look up
    at birches
That move so much in the wind:
Golden rosary sails
    that catch the autumn
    and flex the great boughs,
And then to look down
    to find that this was all a symbol,
A ceremony for us, the living,
    to breathe easier now;
It's just minutes of another day
    and I need this coat to stand it for
Cold is more, now, vivid
    / more painful than grief.

Opalise / Settle

Us curled up in a white cloud,
Chet Baker in a mug on your countertop:
The Lord and Lady, and their bard
Through tinny speakers and cheap crockery;

Temporary doesn't do it for me anymore,
I want to take root / opalise / settle,
I want to put / punch / whack
A nail in the wall.

Yellow

Don't be afraid to paint it as blue as blue can be
   —Gauguin

Dance with me one second
While I unlock our elbows
And pirouette you across me
So you can kick the line of
Almond blossom jetsam
Washed up on the kerb.

You love my eyes,
Or at least how they see /
Or at least what they see /
What I say they see /
How I say what they see:
Dying leaves on branches
That begin their slow embrace
Of the old streetlamp
Whose light manufactures a mock robinia /
Naked twigs wind
A haloing nest occasionally punctured
By astigmatic lines.

We don't actually live our warmth through our eyes
But hold the slide projection mounts
Full of today
Up to November light through the window
And see these gasping stanzas:
Memories cast onto clouds.

The harder the goodbye
The better we are doing,
And our goodbyes are
Of bright gingko tree optimism
Zooming out / spiralling upwards.

On The Day You Were Born
Ezekiel 16 v1–6

A bloody organ specked with earth
That only vultures won't reject
Lay kicking in its afterbirth
And half inhuman with neglect,

Attached by the umbilical
As to a heartless ball and chain
Her every breath's a miracle,
Her every sense is blind in pain.

Galvanistic, futilely
Usurping death's prerogative,
From deep within her rolling sea
She hears the whispered order: 'Live'.

Yoked Cattle, One a Sojourner

        Does something of me
           softly kick the legs
           out from under the anxious,
Press them into the embroidered
           pillows of a low chaise-longue
And take a seat, as I walk
           with them, behind
           their beating mind?

The Folly
Proverbs 25 v28

What these ruins must once have been!
    The visitor can be pleased with the shoulders
Wallowing, rough waves claiming the back,
    The clamour of rooks nesting in the hair,
For he doesn't need to spend the brutal night.

MARIANA PEÑA FEENEY

Mariana Peña Feeney is a multicultural writer and spoken word poet. She has performed at The Poetry Café, for Bath's Literary festival, and at Toast in the Norwich Arts Centre. She lives in East Anglia but was born and raised in Santa Cruz, Bolivia, a city where toborochi trees blossom with pink flowers at the height of winter. Her writing explores identity, otherness, feminism, and that Frank O'Hara-like compulsion to worship the sacred in the ordinary.

Marianapf9@gmail.com

Poems
Ode to a Pink Hat
Only Alice Walker Can Save Me Now
Souls Circle Soho

Ode to a Pink Hat

I bought a pink hat.
They will say that one pink hat is inessential
two pink hats are unfathomably greedy
but three?

A pink hat is freedom so boundless
Like Frank, *I am the least difficult of men.*
all I want is boundless love.
A pink hat is respite so subtle

it is a promise of the coming end
of postponement of self.
Frank would've rejoiced in its possibilities
under trees; Alan — I don't know —

he was more concerned with howls
and the lion in his living room.
You are concerned with luxury
because it is man-made beauty

yet, you yearn for god-made beauty
my sad friend said to me
(we were all sad that May of 2020).
Two continents away he is interpreting a dream I had

last night: in the bathroom mirror
I see a deciduous forest
it sprouts out of my scalp
and a crystal lake shimmers

life efflorescent green and blue.
Alarmed at the flowering
ecosystem on top of my skull
I hide it under a pink shawl

Layers of Liberty prints drape salaciously.
Now I may safely return to the world.
I thought I was done with poetry
but pink hats demand it of me.

May 2020: another bankruptcy announcement.
Does it even matter in context?
My contemporaries will think my grief
for the loss of the inessential

a mark of a hidden shallow nature
but just like Ben Lerner saw the sublime
of Shelley's Mount Blanc in the cereal aisle
I see the eternity of Dickinson's garden

in the fashion department of Bloomingdale's.
A pink hat is a party thrown by the reincarnation
of Oscar Wilde at the Savoy Hotel
on the 50th Anniversary of the first Pride.

How will we know to be proud
now that Pride is cancelled?
Who will teach us to celebrate?

Many thinkers and philosophers will say
this retail apocalypse is a good thing.
Maybe Mr Wilde would have too
and yet —

he would have bought that pink hat
(with debt)
and loved it boundlessly

Only Alice Walker Can Save Me Now[1]

I am of the preference of being my own
sun over being the darling of anyone

suns are unconcerned with value
systems fabricated by fearful homo sapiens

but I am not
what I am
when I am
with them

I am the liquid poured in
that takes the shape of the container
the nebulous grand —

mother's milk: unkind
uncut and bubbling

inside the galactic carafe
sugar will mask only so much
more than you think.

I swear I saw a sun in there
somewhere or two or three.
I am the returning recruit. I am

---

1 After the first eight lines of *Be Nobody's Darling* by Alice Walker
Be nobody's darling;
Be an outcast.
Take the contradictions
Of your life
And wrap around
You like a shawl,
To parry stones
To keep you warm

the 1930s zombie
at vigil inside a bowl of cream
posing as the open sea.

Daughters, come on in,
the water is fine!
I am the only one who replies:

but aren't we lactose intolerant?
Is this love or is this a stomach ulcer?

I am the foam that adorns
the champagne
flutes passed around to the pleased

and respectable members of society.
I am palatable to them all, the darling
of the dinner party

by design I am piquant
in all correct, appropriate
cruel percentages

The sun is nobody's darling
and I am their darling daughter.
You do the math.

I am the words
that curdle then oxidise

behind this gated thunder of a smile.
Beside this hypothermic lullaby.

I ask, was there a sun
around here somewhere?

And is this acid reflux
or is this a solar flare?

Alice Walker told me what not to be
and what to be. Here I am

entreating through repetition;
casting enchantments
for plasma and for density.

I do it for the gut
health. I do it for the warmth

Souls Circle Soho (*scavenging*)

buoyant like
the rings of smoke
stemming from the abyss
between your lips.

London, they spell out:
L-O-N-
      -D-O-N
emphasis on the O's.

Look, it's my last cigarette.
Boys kiss boys. Girls kiss girls.
You reject all of these titles — except
for the title of authority
over what flows

into my superior vena cava.
Your magic tricks, they turned
water to wine and wine to lava.

You spin me —
in circles I embrace all
your dance floor clichés.
Latent, grey, serpentine
this thread

delineating your pupils.
Is it made of mirrors?
Is it made of mercury?

Now it uncoils like
a whisper (or a rattlesnake)
demarcating my entire body.
Look, this is not love
(You remind yourself,

amidst the retching and tears
of fellow strangers)
N-o-t-
    -L-o-v-e
emphasis on the Knot.

Still, it is blinding,
blood stirring, it makes
alphabet soup out
of grey matter.

Flamingo feathers pour
out of these irises like two
iridescent, satin waterfalls. You
let go

of cardboard cut-outs
of human beings evaporating
untouched over and over
again by one another.

CHRISTOPHER PERRY

Christopher Perry writes as he wonders while he wanders.

www.voyageswriting.com
clperry@hotmail.co.uk

Poems
Leopard
False Memory Syndrome
Gymnast
Saturday Afternoon Three O'Clock
We Prefer Happiness
Paul, last heard of in Heaven

Leopard

I had chosen the hotel without any clear idea
of whether I would be taking you back
or putting you in a taxi home

having said goodbye after that dinner
we had caressed from texts
and delicate hours of calls

in which mutual intentions
had been forensically deciphered
or so I thought

until I caught a flash
of frightened girlhood
in your hazel eyes

we just laid beside each other
fully clothed gently tipping
secrets onto the bedspread
where they winked back under
the frost-hard full moonlight

you said *no one has ever done this for me*
before it was always me running around
making others' dreams more probable
and how nice this was

as all you had to do was lie
about your whereabouts
a key skill you worked on as a child
after discovering it enabled escapes
that might keep you safe

it occurred to me then
that naturally a day would come
when telling another
would be more important to you
than telling the truth
to me

False Memory Syndrome

found myself awake alone
you still, asleep head on my arm
what a burden your slender neck must hold
if your resting skull makes my limb grow numb?
how much it weighs with love's strength gone

you lay lids soft; breath lightly feathered
beads of sweat cooling on your brow
a corner crinkled hint of smile

I saw the electrocution of your lashes
as somewhere within shocking pictures played out
on walls of un-locked vaults

strange memories form
in heat of combination
that shift a little with each re-run

watching afternoon's shadows
stretch across the ceiling
I remembered

as we lay collapsed
on wet-patched sheets
that pressed mirrored creases into our skin

that I'd just dreamt
of her. Not you. Not here.

Gymnast

fast feet slap tarmac
car brakes slew vehicle
into boy on the run
for his bus home

where he wants to throw
that blazer on his bed, undo the striped knot
of chocolate and gold tying him
to chalk dust motes
and ink scratched books
and sour sweat of monks
whose god only knows what they see
in the work they do to boys' heads
with their slaps and shouts
in ill-qualified education
of the county's favoured Catholic sons

some of whom wait on the opposite kerb
hear the scream of smoke from sliding tyres
whose faces turn pale as silence falls
birds freeze in flight while they are joined
by his mother's only son cartwheeling
with adidas kit bag diagonally worn
a rotating star as delicate as Olga Korbut
in slowed Munich Olympic motion
along the spine of the still stopping car

he lands on his regulation brown shoes
and runs as fast as fast as fast
he might be granted this second chance
to jump and grasp the steel pole
on the open platform of the No 14
the unknowing driver already
pulling away silently chiding
those bloody kids who make him late

the conductor shakes his turbaned head
not believing what he's just seen
he asks *tickets lads?*
while the gymnast belly laughs at his luck
in catching up with his best mate
who always makes him sing soprano inside
who always beats him to the bus and last seat
who will one day lie in his bed
quite dead before him too

Saturday Afternoon Three O'Clock

'...and in his memory, please stand to pay your respects with one minute's silence, starting on the referee's whistle.'

thousands of clattering seats slap / slap / slap into place
murmuring conversations drift away on the westerly breeze coming off
    the Solent

Fratton End chants stutter then stop

visiting fans decked out in orange and white ease up to stand polite
a lone herring gull cry is caught in the gaping cave of sudden silence
in a flurry of flaps a puffed-up promiscuous pigeon chases his next hen

players stand ranked in semi-circles arms draped over bright coloured
    shirts
behind and beneath the stadium's tiers, chasing up concrete stairs, late
    arrivals rush breathless onto the concourse

loud banter stalls embarrassed by the rigid rows of coats
in row GG, seat 43 a lone tear drawn from its well by recall of passed
    friends fills up then rolls down the long-retired docker's face

a polystyrene coffee cup caught by wisp of wind spirals in a concrete
    gully scutters amplified to all

beyond this cloud of quiet a siren rushes through the city's streets
moist eyes peer through mists toward the man in the middle
who checks his watch raises whistle to lips, draws breath in then blows
    out sharp

on that welcome shrill blast
seventeen thousand four hundred and twenty-six voices
roar out in relief to clear near-choked throats

We Prefer Happiness

en bloc mind guerrillas still write
free verse together

Lennonists who prised open the iron fist
to fit a velvet glove stitched from rusting curtain
imagine *Love is the answer*

but will your umbrellas deflect a typhoon
belting rain, tear gas, rubber bullets
where Opium Wars unfettered colonial trade?

are one hundred Lennon walls innumerate?
two into one will not go

watch how bubbles merge
when we dirty our linen publicly
watch how the island gradually absorbs The North

posting it to The Man with sticky notes
lacks the currency he can afford
a longer view than democracy dictates

I owe my happy home to Hong Kong
& Shanghai Banking Corporation
I accept my freedom is indebted servitude

I draw virtual strength from ignorance
for who can know-it-all?
keep hope! soon the field will be *free from weeds*

occupants of Hong Kong answer me this
(you have as long as it takes to fold your umbrellas)

as Earth moves to extinguish excessive heat
beneath sweltering seas will you still *feel*
that staying human is worth while?

Paul, last heard of in Heaven

        afterwards your mother recalled, when I phoned
        how you had so loved balloons, bright moons
        held on string, they dancing for so long
        as they had breath in their lungs

        you would waltz each one home
        nurse them until they shrank
        shrivelled like your poor father's skin
        you had always chosen balloons over ice cream

        you twigged early on that balloons don't last
        she seemed glad of that, they were cheaper
        (and cleaner) than keeping guinea pigs
        and she noted that the adults don't eat their young

        despite this knowing you sobbed
        at every punctured loss until you stopped
        asking for balloons and grew to find life

        in the arms of men
        some of whom seemed to love you
        no more than balloons

MAX PURKISS

Max Purkiss is twenty-four years old. He grew up in Essex and his favourite poet is Langston Hughes because of his rhythm and rhyme. purkissmax64@gmail.com

Poems
Three Decades From Disaster
Mad as a Mulberry
the answer will come back different and deader each time
Feel The Dead Around You
the hamster hound sound

Three Decades From Disaster

I
2020

Next time you're in the wild strip off clean and go for a swim.
Let a trembling waistline of water
swell above your neck.
Coax goosebumps from their toasty rabbit hole pores.
Open embassies of instinct in your post-barbaric bones.
Have sensation sup the nectar from your nerves.
Wake powerplants of impulse in your flesh.
Send adrenaline snowploughing through your veins.
Don't stop until your head is conkerishly compact,
mucused full with wonder as limbs slacken on the bank
like over-pollinated flowers.
Discard the tiny pandoraless box life's packed you to sleep in
and stand neanderthal-naked on the grass.
Feel the might of mossed green-blooded earth
beneath your little pig-pink toes
and shiver under passing towels of wind.

II
2050

I am wandering a wasteland
rich in steel fruit, affluent in shoots of flame and stone.
herds of wind-up sheep
malfunction while they bleat,
the iron-filing grass has just been mown.
the wind whines from a vent
scattering seeds of cement
which pray for demolition once they're grown.
not one fish ever wakes
in cool formaldehyde lakes,
toy swans creak on their surface all alone.
stuffed birds fly strapped to cables,

wings spread wide by staples,
beaks kept clean by rains of acetone.
one smoggy afternoon
gas-clouds ambushed the moon,
her glossy whereabouts are still unknown.
blue paints slowly dry
on a brand new Perspex sky
to which the sun's been barbarously sewn.

Mad as a Mulberry

It's a funny phrase that. Never knew why Mum said it.
She'd sit back in her rocking chair, or forward on her barstool,
look into the unplugged eyes of whomsoever was polite enough
to register her ramblings and say 'Mad as a Mulberry!'.

The world was mad and people madder. So went the unswerving truck of her
     opinion.
The day she passed I'm sure I heard those syllables crawl up one last time,
roaches out of an egg,
and scribe themselves onto the wind.
m a d   a s a   m u l b e r r y

Her death shrank them
into an osmium nut of mystery.

Her funeral wagged its shaggy tail
loose of mourners,
an understated, underattended affair,
coffin, cafe, cab.

the answer will come back different and deader each time:

love sicks up galaxies in a single star, slices what you never knew was whole. more than swapping sweat. more than a cherry-tubed heart shrieking the juice from its chambers. love is a three-winged bat among birds disguising wonky flight as flamboyance. a conch blackmailed from its shell by dolphin-dense tides, finless glob of longing. love is the lump with leafy wings and torn-out teeth, half bear half butterfly rolling down a stale hill of honey. love is a cloud-surfing sun, rain-rotted and brilliant, chopping ten-tentacled rays like growths from her back. love is the madly swivelling brushes of a car wash leaving dimples in your brain. love is green fog smooching a monochrome garden. love is dyed dishwater swilled down as orange juice. love is the torn out larynx of a fifty foot bluebird pulsing with tumorous song. love is seven sorbets on one spoon. a mistletoed giant stomping on your future. a strawberry-lace-wind lashing your cheeks with snow. a wobbly plank of a plan you walk when nothing else is clear. a rocket taking off back to front and ripping the earth a new core. a chronic crumpling of the chest. a lifelong stare into your favourite face. a visageless voice screaming your shyest beliefs. a moon guarding derelict powerplants. a pair of spectacles collapsing the bridge of your nose. an earthquake napping under sugar-glass houses. mosquito sitting calmly on your heart.
love is smashing like a plate on the platform to catch the first train home.

see. different and deader each time,
a mountain insisting on three or four climbs
before it confesses it's conquered.
no ropes or hooks or abseiling down either,
you have to free fall, brace your spine like a rolled up rug
and pray the cymbaling spank of failure doesn't bruise.

still, what sort of a dung-hearted, tissue-tempered wimp would you be
if you did not write of love?
did not look for it,
did not search – search like a fire through smoke –
scrummage through the nettles of your temper,
skydive from the copters of your joy,
haggle your horizons,
swab your voids
for love.

look for it.
in the shoe polish shine of the sea   in the gut-swirling heat of volcanos
in the greaseless green leaves of the forest   in the unapplied force of a breeze
look for it. it's there.
in the spit of dribbling stars   in the gunpowder dunes of a desert
in the wick-short temper of a storm cloud   can you taste it?

the billion-berried juice of a jungle   the feverish tang of a swamp
the frozen shut legs of a mountain   the cinnamon soul of a rose
look for it. it's there to be found or fumbled.
    take the moon for example. note how she sits, a surly c-list celebrity
   autographing the dusk with chalk. can you hear it? the screech of her nails
                    down sky. there's a bloody wing
scraping off its feathers to try and slip through the narrowing cracks of your heart,
out into a world it's heard so very little about but what little it knows is rapture
                 and spring air jinxing snow
        and flowers smuggled out of soil when frost isn't looking
            and lightning-struck trees shaking their fiery hair.
I promise you it's there.
in the dynamite crash of rejection   in the pipsqueak chaos of a tear
in the tinkling glissando of a smile   in the undisclosed goodness a satellite sees

it was there last time I checked,
jellyfish out of water, happy after death to stay and sting.

you may lose it,
you may find it twice and think it halved
or thrice and think it tripled,
you may think it myth, yesterday's pearl, but it's yours if you're willing to dive.

look for it
wherever you go god damn it
and if you find it, share it.

don't you dare sit, as small as you are smug,
throwing anchors at sinking ships.

wade out to their aid and scramble on deck,
pull every last soul from the wreck,
even those who drowned, check their pulses hours after,
defibrillate the gloom with electric shocks of laughter.
when you first meet a person let them crash into an iceberg of good will.
lift their head by their hair if you have to. origami their world into
warmth.
whitter on till they're listening about a place
where coffins grow from graves and bloom corpses back to life
and all of luck's scorned exes take each other for a wife.
look for it – the squelch of a dew-fat lawn, the sycophant twinkle of a
rainbow –
and if you see it
don't alarm it.
let it think you fell for its disguise,
calmly wave it off into timid turquoise skies.
when the world's half ash half flame
and your heart's one pulse from cracking
it's still with you, flowing over your skin like a golden outer blood.

Feel the Dead Around You

Great sonar-system of souls,
They need not gift you any solid word,
For theirs is a light
That on any given night
Can load a thousand larks inside one cocksure bird.
Feel the dead around you
In warmth as much as shivers,
Feel the dead rush through you
Like many rival rivers,
Feel the dead beneath you
Like Earth's most aching bruise,
Feel the dead deliver
That which life can only lose,
Feel the dead above you
Like a secret second sun,
Feel the dead speak to you
Like a great titanic tongue,
Feel the dead uplift you
Like a million-fingered hand,
Feel the dead at distance
As a ship is seen from land,
Feel the dead afflict you
Like an old bone-kindling curse,
Feel the dead escape you
Like a half-remembered verse,
Feel the dead embrace you
Like a huge transparent twin,
Feel the dead build strength
Across the scaffold of your skin.
Feel the dead around you,
Let them feel you back,
Feel them veer into your veins
Like a crimson Cadillac
But never hold them to the promise of their presence,
For theirs is a tune undecided as the moon
As she wanes and waxes through a thousand crescents.

the hamster hound sound

life gave me a penny when I didn't want any so I threw it off the Eiffel Tower,
some lucky sod caught it and as soon as he touched it the damn thing turned into a flower.

morning gave me the sun when I didn't want one, so I chucked her into outer space,
I should've known better than to mess with her orbit – she slapped a comet back in my face.

the kettle gave me a tea every morning for free, I said 'don't you know your god damn worth?'
she said 'guess I'm a giver, want any sugar?' – 'no wait, put the milk in first!'

the shower spat in my eye so I made the bitch cry, said 'you're gonna lick my butt cheeks clean.'
she said 'I'll do more than that, if you hold back the fat I can even reach up in between.'

my shoe gave me a blister I said 'listen mister, just you stop nibbling my socks.'
he said 'what can I say? a fella goes wolf after twenty-odd years in a box.'

my mouth told a joke and nobody laughed, I said 'you better start making less sense.'
she said 'stop giving me grief and start brushing your teeth (spearmints ain't no great expense).'

my hair pulled a runner, said 'freeze or I'll shoot!', it dropped right down to the floor,
I stuck it with glue and dyed it bright blue but it don't comb the same anymore.

my hand fumbled a cig, the sweaty-palmed pig, I said 'pick the lung-honey up quick!'
she said 'if that's a threat you can take it back yet' then gave her stiff knuckles a click.

my nose did a sneeze, a real lip-soiler, it dribbled down onto my chin,
I whipped out my hanky and gave him a glare, said 'so much for holding it in.'

my stomach churned food in a real bad mood, I said 'come on now missus, be quiet!'
she said 'I'll keep on turning till you get to learning the joys of a half healthy diet.'

my eyes kept on crying, blinking and frying, blurring and wincing and weeping,
I said 'come on now chaps you leaky tear-taps, ain't you supposed to be sleeping?'

my heart caught herpes and all of love's lurgies and coughed each beat dry in my chest,
I said 'chill in your chambers you silly old bat and don't make no bed for a guest!'

my soul sucked a bong of its mystical pong, then slumped on the nearest couch cushion,
she woke to a sound half hamster half hound catcalling from inside her bosom.

GEORGE RICHARDS

George Richards writes in the field of environmentalism and nature, seeking ways to process, and face up to, ecological flux today. He is a writer and editor at *Bloom in Doom*, a positive, solution-based ecological journal. He studied Literature at the University of Exeter and spent a year teaching English in Hong Kong before coming to do his MA in Norwich.

george.richards388@gmail.com

Poems
The Music Was Beautiful During the Plague
Forest Fire
Lovebird
Dragonflies

The Music Was Beautiful During the Plague

Dead of winter. Plague came & scared away
the birds. Leaves on the trees, unblooded. Whole streets
pearling at the edges we couldn't touch, we stacked
bottleflies as they died under the stairs in mothdust.
Winter followed winter. Through the windows,
we watched a crow falling apart on the driveway.
Each morning, the road disappeared
down its long sloppy throat.

I learnt as a boy you can't save every
broken animal that howls & keeps the town up.
But also how wonder sometimes creaks inside us.

Some nights, we pressed our ears
to the walls and listened to the trapped music
coming from the flats behind us.

Not everything we put out into the universe
can come straight back to us, I know, but the music
was beautiful, even in the plague.

Forest Fire

All at once
dead branches shuttering the green
clearings overgrowing at the edge of the wood
where the match is dropped,
its small light spilling across the rot to nudge
oaks out of root

/

last hurried notes of the finches leaving their graces behind,
their sodden wings chopping up sky
to slip out of a wind that lifts
this small puddle of light

/

up close
a sunslide in back-motion buffers open,
sporing up its frontmist
into thick air

/

then the sintering
which yokes the eye and trips you up and dries the river
dragging its sound of ocean breaking
through the wood

/

wind wincing it sideways into
new shapes to eat pine and oak,
smoke flowers holding onto the drought, the decomposing,
bodying it across the spot you stand on
and spluttering up into what dark

what clearing the throbbing eye can hardly hold
hardly unthroat or twist out of

/

an eye heavy with longing,
you only see five steps ahead,
smoke drips from the leaves,
cut tongues all drained
of colour

/

colour of shelled-out bloodshot
holding onto blood. yours and the forest's.
both are emptying.

Lovebird

Lovers pour oil into each other's eyes.

Shadows vine across the pavements
in front of their house.

Picture the house
weathered by the washed colours
of a June that has come for them.

Picture the house
unrendered at first and then swelling under
a bruised dusk the light pollution sucks
into focus.

Picture a door.

Picture the door opening slowly
and all that oil streaming out into silted air.

The lovers have been talking to each other
in their sleep.

He hasn't been happy.

Try harder, little bird, she said to him
but he couldn't stop thinking

how lonely another lover
with lovely bones looked.

He kept chasing her breath
through the streets in loops,
his eye shuttering to take everything in.

Picture the evening
pulling everything back
like an eye caught in the sway of an oil spill.

Picture the city
rising up from oil slicks and sucking
all the land in.

Picture the bedroom snowing

him rushing through the house
switching on all the lights

her remembering the true story
of the lonely boy with lovely bones
who nailed her throat to his lovebite
all those months ago.

Snatched from focus
the city swallows
trains, birds.

Back in focus, the lovers swallow ice
and cut to black.

There is so much oil in the river.

Cut to black.

Dragonflies

Down by the river, the open vein of it,
a boy threads through water
looking for dragonflies.
Shadows slack on larches where he tries to trace
decay chains coiling between
white roots and piling up. Larvae
stridulate off the roots crimping at the edge
like old bones or dead coral.
Oil on water globes out in long
chords he tries to trace but the body keeps
getting in the way. The river keeps slipping.
Lichen stains remembering
his chemical composition.
The body's drought cresting the nerves
of pinheads. He used to listen
but can't anymore
to the sounds this leaking body makes.
This is the silent shuffle
of chemical after chemical in his skull.
The *click click click* of the ice thawing.
Irregular heartbeats
& no dragonflies.

JESSE SMITH

Jesse Smith is a queer poet. They primarily write on gender and sexuality, and their interplay with the body and language. Their work has been published by Stone of Madness Press and Delicate Friend, and they can be found on Twitter and Instagram @jesse_poet.

jesse_poet@outlook.com

Poems
empty, except for
ages through the bedroom
excavation; disorder
my gender
duplex

empty, except for[2][3]

cw: menstruation, blood, genitalia, deadnaming, war rhetoric

unnoticed, until the flood of its removal labelled *failure* from a body labelled *female*. solitary. like a word forbidden in the throat. longing to unfurl into a tongue, like a body before a body before a reckoning, like *label* is the autonomy of a tongue, the laying of a kiss on something you can't otherwise touch, unless it's the furling of *female* around an outlier (like *outlier* is a word escaping the tongue) the close of *empty* like lips into a silence unlike a kiss which is a reckoning unlike language, the knotting of tongue into a deadname and womb into a reinstatement. you think: shrapnel. i think: undetonated. i think: *male*, repackaged before it can be known. like *empty* is like a swallow. i reckon these fem-slicked muscles like tongues furling like lovers into a reckoning.

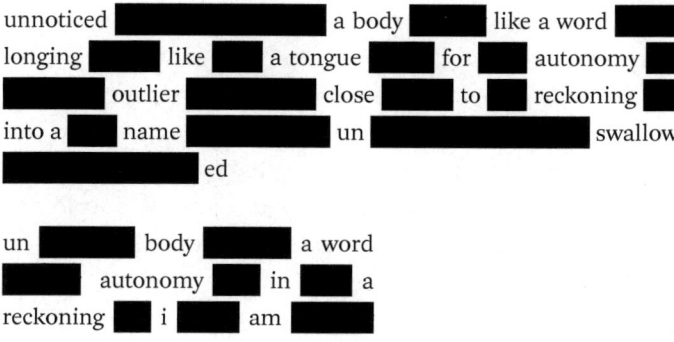

---

2 Inspired by the Escapril 2021 Day Three prompt: 'empty, except for ___'.
3 The 'burning haibun' form is by torrin a. greathouse, as debuted in her debut collection *Wound from the Mouth of a Wound* (Milkweed Editions, 2020).

ages through the bedroom

cw: implication of abusive/unaccepting household, violence (not bodily), gender dysphoria, brief misgendering of self

I sketch a smiley face onto the wall beside my bed, like a mirror. I blink and the wall is purple. It bleeds through the paint, it doesn't. My eyes remember, fingers search for the bump, forget. Smile, purple, bed frame. The bed at this angle, I cry myself to sleep. I'm still a girl at this angle. The mirror on the wardrobe, I'm seen to gather my hair into a ponytail, stretch my tight-slicked thighs out from under the skirt, the yearbook gathering dust like forget. The mirror at another angle, I kiss a girl and see the remembering at once. A girl, a boy, a no-longer. I'm hoping there's a boy at another angle. The doorknob fits its dent in the wall, it makes it deep as your anger, caved as the voice. Purple. As the self in the body in the mirror. I turn and carve a boy out of that jaw, a smile out of the dark like a future. I'm crying – I'm in love and I'm heartbroken. You see me, you don't. The bed at two angles, spanning two walls, into a corner, at the same angle I write my first story of boys in love and the boy that lives in my throat, waiting this room out. I cry enough tears to strip the purple from these walls, I cry enough to make myself transparent. I'm dreading a thousand mornings in one night, restless for one.
I hold each instance
of myself in this breath –
we've all been waiting.

excavation; disorder

cw: disordered eating, excessive thinness, body horror, gender and genital dysphoria, mention of genitalia, mention of death

        the *boy*
    of me has always been
        within
  this *body*, smothered –
         so i
  let the body eat itself
        away:
   its bloody whinging
        turns
 to dry wrings of self-
       chisel
-ling out the sharp boy
        jaw,
 draining of the pretty
        pink
 from this skin, i own
       scars
 of its fizzling-down as
     a mark
 of reclamation – if i
      starve
 it out enough, will it
       suck
 its fat from my chest,
       will i
 get to upchuck that
       sack
that swole my hips and
       used
 to salivate? this boy
      heart
 beats to be seen; if
       boy

         means bringing my
              body
        to the brink of its
             death,

my gender[4]

dust beneath my feet. My gender is the way skin leaves me to crumble away. My gender never dies, even when it leaves me. It leaves me like shrapnel, like tears – when there's excess that my body can't contain, but never runs out of. My gender overflows. My gender comes out in strong language. It rages. My gender is the child in me that is finally able to grow. It's a fossil in reverse. It's unbreakable. My gender lulls in my sleep, curls up against my partner and weeps. It weeps in joy against my partner. My gender breaks bread. My gender shakes cis hands with caution. It thrifts. It gulps down lines from Ocean Vuong, torrin a. greathouse, danez smith, it keeps a pen between its teeth. Cracks it, lets it flow. My gender writes me love notes. It writes and passes me DO YOU WANNA BE MY BOYFRIEND? YES NO. Its feet swing just off the floor. It snatches it back, scrawls, passes it back: I WANT TO GET TO KNOW YOU FIRST. My gender is the dust I kick into eyes. Gather into snowballs, into a figure. I kick it up into a cloud, shape a name, shower. My gender whispers. It itches. It tugs at my skin. Finally, I let my body touch it. Sink into the warm bath of it. My gender yawns, stretches its

---

[4] Inspired by a prompt from London Queer Writers in their Writing Queer Utopias workshop (8th April 2021).

duplex[5]

cw: misgendering, mention of death / transphobic violence, blood, violence, implied menstruation

my daughter is dead my mum will say
but i know her name will warm the lips

of a body whose blood stirs *girl*, unleaving
yet. we swap names in the dark

like love notes. in here, i can kiss
this name like a prayer to my knuckles

which kiss her own name to her lips
like lipstick. we dreamed of our graves

engraved with these names – is there
where is gets us? *until* is a grave

we're digging ourselves out of, the closet
the closest we'll get to ourselves, else

closing a hand round the throat. in
here, i think, a grave in its bud.

---

5 The 'duplex' form is by Jericho Brown, as debuted in *The Tradition* (Copper Canyon Press, 2019).

TIM SNELL

Tim Snell is an English-language teacher based in South Korea. Before teaching, he lived and worked with a community of homeless people in London. He is currently writing a collection of poetry which explores Bildung and human flourishing. It is provisionally titled 'Yolks and Goo and $CaCO_3$' – or, in other words, 'eggs'.

timdsnell@outlook.com

Poems
An Ache
Gin-in-tonic had licked its hairline–

An Ache

I squash my feet against the floor,
they are like grilled tomatoes or pressed ham.
Limbs carry this flesh, but bones carry limbs,
and these my bones they ache.

I hear machine: a jargon noise
recurring, a screech without
climax, a string of *ee* looping *ee,*
but these my bones they ache.

And the ache is waffling:
it makes no point that needles,
has no finger-traceable shape –
it's a shapeless ache that's somehow bloomed.

Would that it could slide
like small talk into lullaby,
like the sand that was caught in a turtle's claws
and now lays on the bed of a pellucid sea.

But I squash my feet against the floor,
they are like grilled tomatoes or pressed ham;
and these my bones they ache,
and these my bones they ache.

Gin-in-tonic had licked its hairline–

    fracture limbs, but the fly took off from the lip
    of the highball glass. i thought, 'That one sound

    it makes is made of two: *flit* and *flut*'.
    The flow of the tongue has my testament: i say *flit*
    and the tongue arches up on the vowel, i say *flut*

    and it retracts.   *flit-flut fli-fluh li-luh i-uh i-uh*
    Flies ball these vowel sounds into
    a fuzzy diphthong, but all we say is *i-uh.*

    We can ball other sounds, such as
        ah———ee
      ah——ee

            ah—ee
                    ah-ee   I
    but is there any fuzz in that?

                    ————

    i hankered for a flight helmet
    when i was young and gunning for steam
    as if it were the I

    i could slip into.
    And with a waft of my fisherman's net,
    (for I've always been a fisherman),

    with a waft of my fisherman's net,
    i clicked and joined the fighter pilots'
    chat group. There, a square photo of an Apache

    helicopter, stocked with squatting
    projectiles, had written
    a touchpaper comment in plain font:

'to be honest mate I just wanna
get sum dirty ***** in my sights haha'

And sub-comments whizzed
around it, a juggling
of sparking

rectangular fervour
like their *haha* bulletins
recapping their racist *hahas*.

I would have
ducked
like an extra in a cowboy movie,

but X was clicked,
I was gone,
and out of that carapace

i came.
Evidently alone
and doubly so:

a lone crustacean
and not all one;
a thumb's ruby skin

amid some dead-skin curls.

———————

There was more between us
than the sum
of a language.

They spoke as if a heard phrase
was the gift of a thought,
as though to think was Sisyphean.

They spoke English, were English,
but didn't trawl
like an Englisher. And so,

i passed them by
with my bullet-holed net:
i don't know their tessellation game

and I don't know it too.
I'll be at the rockpool,
crabbing.

If it's said I'm lonely there,
say it's my solitude,
for if somewhen ages and ages hence,

I'm blinded, deaf and have numbed nerves
that take nothing from a kiss,
I'm still gonna be out for that sound i heard.

It had a perforating fuzz
and scored a fly with its flit-flut,
it was the sound of a fly in flight

and that of a true true-🖤

KIERA SUMMER

Kiera Summer is a writer of poetry and prose with a BA in French and Arabic from Cambridge University. She is currently writing to explore attachment, addiction, and intergenerational temporality, including a pamphlet: *Notes on the Possibility of Drowning* and a novel: *The Therapeutic Value of Ecstasy (Contact High)*.

kierasummer@cantab.net

Poems
a cuisle
I am almost certain
Meditation
Night-time Invitational
Apology for this ruthless keratin

a cuisle*

A thousand stoves burning through the night and
Sheep fur charring shepherdess and spooled meaning spoiled meaning
Spinning liberal smoke ashing saying go
An accent is a sign of two mothers
Not
    Of two
        Tongues
            In one mouth
But two in the ears going in
    Rather than out.
I idolise thee
Who art in heaven
queen deserter
    Suitcase stowed and under beds
Immigrant dust bunny climbing the spidery
Wretched ascendant ladder in tights and heels
Grandmother
    Mammy
Compromising
    With English vowels   a halfway method of calling
Grandmother doing crosswords in your chair & eating toffees
Fastest knitter in Thiobraid Árann
Who where you then?
Hustling crackle of those firey togs
Finery thwacked and spat at your back knitting
Loins, ovum in ovum in ovum
I heard your
voice
crisp two-part song
I wore your
    Girdle
And it scraped my skin off
I burned it in the sun
As you burned in the sun
I burned in the sun with the ratchety flame
I took the baton for confirmation

Crucifix at your throat
Rode it out into the snow
A milky
horse
Ran my fingers over the yellow flower
And felt the thorns to be ready
Grandmother
Brustig ort
Grandmother
Boated it to the midlands for a job in Air Lingus
A creature of air and silk full of bobbins and pin
money
Pens rolling across the powdered faces
Of tables
Pregnant soon with business
Man grey suits pray tailored red
Rosary necked
Gluey strawberry filled choc-o-lates
She loved life
No one goes a thousand miles to live
    Who doesn't want
        To live
    No one puts it all up in the air
Who can help it
    Grandmother
Quickly weighted with babies
Husbanded into bank accounts
Ink-stained cottons
Catching at her strings
1960s promise passing in a nighty   blur
Inaccessible through thick
Linen under-skirts
Bottle-fed babes sleeping on their backs
Count to ten
Before you get them
    Listen
It all outs
    in the wash
Confession a rag dipped in

Liquor and holy water
Reams of strong secret
    Poems
On the backs of your hands
Washed off while
Cotton woolling
The babies
rash
    I may never understand how you lived not showing
    I have a feeling you carried
in your body
    Rows
of gaelic stitches and names layer caking
sutures of stick rocks and rolls of doily things
    unsewn
I know,
    you died, I began
To baste the hems,
I have them now, I'm wearing them.

---

* A cuisle translates as 'oh darling', though its literal meaning is 'oh pulse' or 'oh vein'.

I am almost certain

    I don't have money to dispose of in salons anyway   there the scissor snip snips me
at the nape   I am a floating head above the black furry bedsheet   silver by my left ear   and I am a city fox screaming
I will not   be pruned
     you made a fruit of me   your spiky balding peach of a body
I hate to think of you near now
skunk breath rank and spitting   how many women let you into the boudoir in the form of wax and clippers   draped you round their mother's necks   called you   *a nice boy*
you are the cutter   clitoridected   your fingers make me seasick   your advice that I find   a skilful Brazilian   or Hollywood   your winking lack of shame   rather pride in
  the desire   to rip me
               how many men took us   by the ponytail the bunch the bun the ringlet
               and dragged us from the rooms   when our voices rose too steeply   still I will not remove myself   this unrelenting vulpine pelt these clothes from my scalp careening   I suggest you return my brush and swiftly leave my bed
           my hair is growing faster since you left

Meditation*

I'm still sad about the years I was no one.
this is a religion. for some.
to do away with. self, for a time I.
hailed Mary statue of lichen. in place of heart, blue cloth, my sin.
nailed myself crosswise & called it wisdom.
I hung there, bloodlessly, bruising.
counting breaths and claiming I was 'thinking'.
every afternoon as a child. my mother would take.
'a little lie down'. there under folds of azure.
shut her, me out. playing at being dead.
ghostly spectre, selfless. Angel at rest.
hosanna with no words. yes. my mother spread-eagled.
pickled liver, Prometheus.

* (with each period read as a stop a clap or a breath.)

Night-time Invitational

Come with me to the dream world
            I know you've been   sad
                                obsess
                                                  scareful at night and
                                  neglect
            that's why I'm inviting you
Let's walk where gold shells
are strewn
            All the oysters rotten
A pantryful of eaten
Fleas in the roost
Let's be the hand in hand crying for our mother's back
Begging god to demask
The shifting man behind the wardrobe
To take his weight off us
            To make the hands
of our lovers more confident
Less muscle fast
Tell me about the way your dreams are all of dying
            One time, a hoop of barbed wire locks your lip
Another he stabs you stabbing him and the red hot
Blood drips and drips
            On the pathway we'll trawl together though the rat bones
Vainglorious buttons
Each one a door way to the
Unpressed
Next time, you pass through that gelatinous curtain
Your hair has been trailing for miles,
Strangelingly beautiful and caught
Let's walk where our childhoods walked
Down in the burrows and hollows
            I know we both lived in the crevices
And crooked crow's feet below lids those pierced past eyeballings
Cavernous hook of each father's elbow the cup of the harsh word's reach
I know you like me have feared
            blood and often fainted

At the sight of one person's loving another
   Like something not of this earth

Apology for this ruthless keratin

I'm sorry now I no longer account for, your strange jealousies,
the locks you begged me pick and unpick,
the dusty stitches, twelve in rows at the front of the head
the blood matting, red, up too in the nails, in bed,
I confess, I too, have run
my hands over them and felt the stinging
bastard, nettle of a man, still reaching for the neck,
I'm sorry the way the cuts were all for you,
the way they did and didn't scalp me too.
I'm sorry to be the open mouth guppy, the scream,
the kind that means there's nothing.
I'm sorry now for the promises, wig safe but could not return,
the unmailed letters of sad, the buried clump of it,
the hair on both of us pulled, scraping by,
I refuse though not to pity myself, when I'm unhappy,
my hair still grows in wealthy curls. I refuse to be wise all the time.

TRISTAN·E

tristan·e is a writer and performer based in London. Their work has featured in numerous journals, films, galleries and live events internationally, and in 2019 they were shortlisted for the Bridport Poetry Prize. tristan·e is the 2020/21 recipient of the *Ink, Sweat and Tears* scholarship on UEA's MA Creative Writing Poetry.

tristanethepoet@gmail.com

Poems
The Silent Veil
Family Portrait
Marry Me When You Meet Me
Morning Routine
Heartquake 101
The Memory of Blood

The Silent Veil

onyx pall
b r i g h t ening
· dot
between thread ·
 by
· dot between
  thread ·
by bit by tiny bit
by just a speckle
and a wish
of air in
a light shift
from quiet dark
      to an umbrous
    echoing down
     of the silent veil
un do ing itself   in whispers
    reviving
        to a kissing world
through w i d e
      o p e n   t e a r s

Family Portrait

```
                    c h e e s e g r i n

                formed of a c r a c k e d  m i rr or
          b u r st ing
                   pieces  dancing
        like  fences
                    ripped up in
             a twister  and  slicing
                     the sky
         into an     ava  av
            a   a    lan   al
           val   v  che    an
           an    a          che
           ch   la   a
            e   nch  v
                e    a
                    la
                     n          of
                    che             m e
                                      m o
                                       r i
                                        e s
                     such that
             the hush
                of your v o i c e
                        seeps from
                        a flower's eye


           such that your flashing through the c l o u d s
            irrev oca bl y
                        d  i
                       s a  p
                          p    e
                              a
                                r
                                 s
```

188

Marry Me When You Meet Me

you smile emoji   switch
to last seen   the absence

of a full stop
meant   everything

offline   i keep checking
over   my history

will show you're who
i want to log into

while i fill up the night on cookies
from dream houses

(note to self: get job)

with room for the personal
data we'll collect

but dawn is bad
for digestion   everything

laid   on a bare
morning buffet

disconnecting   don't go

because liking my freckle shot
means you love me

and if that weren't true
you wouldn't need this much

sleep right   because loving me is sooooo
click to buy right now

and so worth being
   weary

that when your status says
you've woken up

(note to self: check status)

i can't wait
to tell you my last name

Morning Routine

Wipe down the mirror
· concealer ·   —m a s c ara—

my father comes out through a cough
mother   poking up in a hunger pang

i have   to empty   them both
out   to become

            someone   i am
            not
            and could   be

                    but   fuck me if
            i
            i*den*tity is a   c
               e   s   cle r   c
               n   s   e   cut
               t   a   t
               i   r
               t
                 y
                        g
                        e
                        m
s p a r k l i n g   in
God's
    t e e t h

i might see it   when They grin

or when i   fuck me   grin
                        starve
                  cough
                                 conceal

        wipe down the mirror

or mouth   some
        name i didn't choose

    or s q u int a
        G od's
                s
            m   e
                i   L   ʟ of a morning
            .

Heartquake 101

core
of
gold
steel
suspended   arms
from
the rattle rattle r a t t l e
shock shooting up the spine to somewhere
around heart height shock shooting up the scaly spine
r a t t l e – r a t t l ing core of gold hung in steel suspense
caught in the shocked spine r a t t l ed arms that cradle the arms catching
around the scaly spine at heart height and cradle suspended
the golden core rattlin g down
arms bestilling arms at heart height
cradling suspense until the world
sitting gold again
core hung
suspended
in steel
arms
still and
cradled
finally
can

b r ee e ea t h e

out

The Memory of Blood

      is where i break
        beneath a p a s s i n g train
              br e
   a
      k
    i
      n g
b   r   e a   k
    i n   g   crac kled
and s m e a r e d a l o n g t h e t r a c k s
     like grated cherries

                is in waiting
     for finger bits to twitch   to signal out
  to   themselves   *heal*

     is in the tap
      tap
            and jolt
shot foot to heart
in the pulse of lightning
    unforgetting and   L O
                 D O
                  E P
    like
    a nightmare

  so how long   precisely
for a skull to s w e e p
   its pieces back
       into a head?

how long is a piece of broken skin?

ALEX WOOD

Alex Wood graduated from University of the Arts London in 2008 with a BA in Photography. He has since worked as a producer for editorial and advertising campaigns and now spends a lot of time cycling around Suffolk, where he currently lives and writes.

alexwood_1985@hotmail.com

Poems
Seven Buttons
The Driver
Symmetry
Motion Parallax

Seven Buttons

If only you could see
how finely I slice the onion now,
slowly to be sure.

When all this is over
I will probably look back and wonder
if you meant it, wearing your shirt like that.

The Driver

        fixes me with the eyes of a father
        who sees his son does not look well.

        Handing over the gift of how to peel an orange
        he cautions *eat only half.*

        I tell him I am grateful, that I am as tired as an oak
        full of flight and splitting down the middle

        but quite sure that we will be on time so please,
        look at me again, tell me about your son.

Symmetry

I showed you the lark
or how to hear it first
looking upward

we watched it climb
there, then not there
until we lost sight

to bright reverberations
ourselves ascending?
you asked. Not quite

but consider the gap
already less distinct,
no longer who but what.

Motion Parallax

the light
 is yellow
  perfect for collecting
   dust   I remain very still
    close one eye
     and see
      a robin   bend backwards
             in song
              downstairs
               it is harder to keep warm
                everything moves   with the weight of a spoon   I am
                                on the verge of saying something
                                 a line from Housman
                                  anything will do

ACKNOWLEDGEMENTS

Thanks are due to the School of Literature, Drama and Creative Writing at UEA in partnership with Egg Box Publishing, part of UEA Publishing Project, Ltd., for making the MA Creative Writing anthologies possible.

We would also like to thank our tutors over this year for their guidance and understanding: Sophie Robinson, Jeremy Noel-Tod, Meryl Pugh and Tiffany Atkinson.

We are grateful for the hard work of Shannon Clinton-Copeland, Nathan Hamilton and Philip Langeskov at the UEA Publishing Project, and for the essential design and typesetting work of Emily Benton.

Thank you to the editorial committee for putting this year's anthology together:
    Alex Innocent
    Maya Hough
    Sarah Crowe.

With grateful thanks to all the funders who support the scholarships that support our poets, in particular:
    The Ink, Sweat and Tears Scholarship
    The Birch Family Scholarship
    The Bryan Heiser Memorial Scholarship.

UEA MA Creative Writing Anthologies: Poetry

First published by Egg Box Publishing, 2021
Part of the UEA Publishing Project Ltd.

International © retained by individual authors

This book is sold subject to the condition that it shall not, by way of trade or otherwise, be lent, resold, hired out, stored in a retrieval system, or otherwise circulated without the publisher's prior consent in any form of binding or cover other than that in which it is published and without a similar condition including this condition being imposed on the subsequent purchaser.

A CIP record for this book is available from the British Library
Printed and bound in the UK by Imprint Digital

Designed by Emily Benton Book Design
emilybentonbookdesign.co.uk

Proofread by Sarah Gooderson

Distributed by NBN International
10 Thornbury Road
Plymouth
PL6 7PP
+44 (0)1752 202 301
e.cservs@nbninternational.com

ISBN 978-1-913861-26-1